CALIFORNIA NATURAL HISTORY GUIDES

# INTRODUCTION
# TO WATER IN
# CALIFORNIA

# California Natural History Guides

Phyllis M. Faber and Bruce M. Pavlik, General Editors

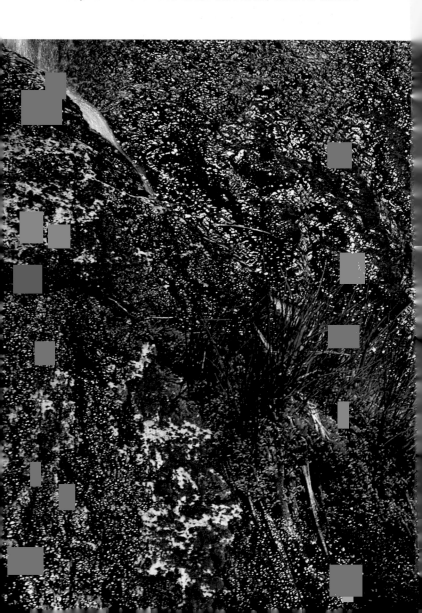

# Introduction to
# WATER IN CALIFORNIA

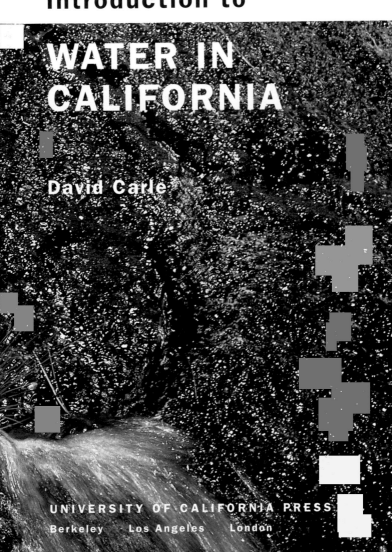

David Carle

UNIVERSITY OF CALIFORNIA PRESS

Berkeley  Los Angeles  London

# California Natural History Guides No. 76

University of California Press
Berkeley and Los Angeles, California

University of California Press, Ltd.
London, England

© 2004 by the Regents of the University of California

Library of Congress Cataloging-in-Publication Data

Carle, David, 1950–.
    Introduction to water in California / David Carle.
        p. cm.—(California natural history guide series; 76)
    Includes bibliographical references and index.
    ISBN 0–520-23580-0 (hardcover : alk. paper).—ISBN 0–520-24086-3 (pbk. :
alk. paper)
    1. Water-supply—California.   2. Hydrology—California.   3. Water-supply—
California—Management.   I. Title.   II. Series.

TD224.C3C3723 2004
363.6'1'09794—dc22                                    2003061246

Manufactured in China
10   09   08   07   06   05   04
10   9   8   7   6   5   4   3   2   1

The paper used in this publication meets the minimum requirements of
ANSI/NISO Z39.48–1992 (R 1997) (Permanence of Paper). ♾

*Cover:* Mill Creek in Lundy Canyon.

The publisher gratefully acknowledges the generous
contributions to this book provided by

the Gordon and Betty Moore
Fund in Environmental Studies
*and*
the Heller Charitable
and Educational Fund

# CONTENTS

# ACKNOWLEDGMENTS

My thanks go to Dorothy Green for her review of the manuscript and for suggesting my name to UC Press when it decided to add a book on water to the long list of titles in the California Natural History Guide series. Thanks, also, to Rita Schmidt Sudman, executive director of the Water Education Foundation, who reviewed the manuscript. The foundation's field trips and publications, including its Layperson's Guides to every aspect of California water, are excellent sources of balanced information. Anyone interested in this subject will benefit from its materials and educational programs. Frances Spivey Webber, executive director of the Mono Lake Committee, also reviewed the manuscript, as did committee cofounder Sally Gaines. Hydrographer Rick Kattelmann, Ph.D., was another reader who provided helpful comments and corrections; he also made several excellent photographs available as illustrations.

Sources for illustrations have been cited, but I must particularly acknowledge the helpfulness of fisheries scientist Tina Swanson and hydrologist Peter Vorster of the Bay Institute; Arya Degenhardt, communications director for the Mono Lake Committee; Rebecca Boyer, with the Department of Water Resources photographic collection; Michele Nielsen, San Bernardino County Museum archivist; Siran Erysian, GIS specialist for the U.S. Bureau of Reclamation; Norma Craig, who handles the Yosemite National Park slide archives; Barbara Beroza and Linda Eade, with the Yosemite Library; Richard Harasick of the Los Angeles Department of Water and Power; Joseph Skorupa with U.S. Fish and Wildlife; and photographer Frank Balthis. The staff at the Water Resources Center Archives at UC Berkeley, as always, were very accommodating.

Many agencies post online information that was helpful in preparing both text and tables, but I also appreciate the personal responses to my questions from the Coachella Valley Water District, San Bernardino Valley Municipal Water District, Desert Water Agency (in Palm Springs), Mojave Water Agency, Santa Clara Valley Water District, and Solano County Water Agency.

As I finished this book, the Department of Water Resources was preparing the next update to the California Water Plan. For the 2003 update, DWR expanded the role of interested members of the public, with open planning meetings and summaries sent to an extended review committee. I thank DWR for adopting that participatory process.

With all this expert help, any errors that slipped by are the author's alone.

I particularly appreciate the suggestions and diligence of copyeditor Lynn Golbetz. Thanks, once again, to Julie Popkin, my longtime literary agent.

Janet Carle, my wife, the first reader of all my books, has saved other readers from an overabundance of commas and my occasional slips into murky prose. This book is dedicated to Janet, who keeps me on track.

# INTRODUCTION
## Water Web: Connected Californians

A California family returned home from a summer outing. Their favorite beach had been posted with closure signs because of contaminated water, but they had found another spot down the coast. Now there was a rush for the bathrooms; toilets flushed several times, then the daughter claimed the first shower. While Mom loaded sandy bathing suits and towels into the washing machine, Dad began rinsing lettuce, tomatoes, and fruit at the kitchen sink. Their son was out in the driveway, energetically hosing salt spray off the family car. Sudsy water ran down the driveway into the sidewalk gutter, eventually falling into a nearby storm drain.

Mom mixed up a pitcher of iced tea and then settled onto a lounge chair beside the swimming pool. Opening bills, she read aloud to Dad (as he put hamburgers on the grill) from a water company insert titled "The Water We Use Each Day."

"It took eight gallons of water to grow one of those tomatoes you just sliced," she told her husband. "That burger patty you're holding took 616 gallons! And my cotton jeans represent 1,800 gallons of water."

Dad started a sprinkler going on the lawn and noticed that the swimming pool level was down. The weather was warm and dry, and the kids' pool party had splashed plenty of water out the day before.

"Landscaping consumes about half the water Californians use at home," Mom added, still reading. "Toilets use 20 percent and showers, another 18 percent."

"Our water meter must be spinning like crazy right now," Dad said, wondering when their daughter would emerge from the shower.

About six weeks earlier, a snow patch had finished melting near the summit of a Sierra Nevada mountain peak. Liquid and flowing again, after five months in cold storage, the water soaked into the ground and began to percolate downhill, pulled by gravity. Nearby tree roots absorbed much of it, but the rest eventually seeped out into a small creek at the base of the hill. The sun and wind evaporated a bit of the water. Animals drank a bit. Some passed through a trout's mouth and gills, losing dissolved oxygen and carrying off a bit of carbon dioxide.

For millennia, water that traveled along this particular part of the water cycle had cascaded down the steep eastern face of the Sierra Nevada, carving a canyon as it went, and finally entered a salty inland sea called Mono Lake. Algae, brine shrimp, and millions of birds took advantage of that oasis in the desert. From there water had nowhere to go but up, reentering the atmosphere by evaporation, to someday fall again as rain or snow. But now, much of this snowmelt was diverted into an aqueduct. It began a 350-mile trip southward, finally reaching a storage reservoir in Los Angeles.

In Southern California it was mixed with other water that had followed even longer routes. Some had originated in snowfields on the western slope of the Sierra Nevada. As that water approached San Francisco Bay via the Sacramento River and Bay-Delta, it was diverted southward into the California Aqueduct. Saltier water traveled up to 1,400 miles from the Colorado River watershed in the Rocky Mountains. Water pumped out of the ground from a local Southern California aquifer joined the mix. That groundwater carried industrial contaminants, but at levels deemed acceptable when diluted.

Now, the water that had entered the Los Angeles Aqueduct system a month earlier was inside a pipe, poised before the water meter of a Southern California home. Each time there was a surge of movement, the meter measured the flow and water moved off through pipes toward the bathrooms, kitchen, laundry room, and yard spigots.

The water from the Eastern Sierra snowfield took its turn sliding past the meter, paused, crept forward, and then began to ooze into the open. A single drop slowly gathered weight at the mouth of the kitchen faucet. At last it fell, straight into the drain. From there, it headed down toward the city's sewage treatment plant. Soon it would return to the sea.

That faucet continued steadily dripping, as it had been doing for many weeks. Another six gallons of water, laboriously harvested from distant environments, dripped down the drain by the end of that day.

An intricate system of dams, aqueducts, and pipes delivers water to people in California. Though water is the essential molecule supporting life on Earth, it can be taken for granted so long as the distribution system quietly works behind the scenes and the California climate cooperates with "normal" weather. Yet the movement of water across the landscape to serve human needs has consequences where water originates and where it emerges from faucets. A full appreciation of today's thoroughly "plumbed" California should foster understanding of the consequences that individual behaviors or community decisions bring for all who share California's water.

Consider how difficult it must be for someone in Los Angeles, "at the far end of the pipe," to realize the connection between a few gallons of water thoughtlessly wasted—or carefully conserved—each day, and populations of birds on a salt lake 350 miles away. An environmental battle was fought in the courts and in the arena of public opinion for 16 years over damage caused to Mono Lake, an inland sea east of Yosemite National Park, by stream diversions to Los Angeles. After visiting Mono Lake and seeing it teeming with migratory birds, many tourists are amazed that anyone in California ever opposed complete protection for such a national treasure. Yet the distant, unseen impacts are hard to perceive for millions of urban water users making individual daily choices.

When a new subdivision is built in an urban area, do planners and developers, or the families that move into those houses, appreciate the connections being made? Water must reach each household through a network of dams, aqueducts, water treatment plants, and delivery pipes. Some water may travel nearly 700 miles from the upper watershed of the Feather River in Northern California. Another branch of the water system extends 1,400 miles up the Colorado River to its headwaters in the Rocky Mountains of Colorado and Wyoming, so that the winter weather of those distant states has become more significant to many Californians' annual water supply than local rainfall.

Federal, state, and local agencies operate systems that tie Californians together through their web of water pipes. Water availability shaped the state's urban growth and development. Extensive aqueduct systems enabled population increases far beyond what regional water limits would have allowed. Those large populations generated wastes and industrial pollutants that have moved into groundwater basins, rivers, and lakes, and diminished trust in the quality of the water emerging from our taps. Looking for more water to serve unceasing demands, urban water interests today covet supplies committed to California agriculture. The state's farms feed much of the nation, but they face pressure and financial incentives to market or transfer their water to domestic uses.

The environment remains the ultimate source for water. California has a tremendous range of climates and hydrologic conditions. Snow on the Sierra Nevada becomes the state's largest "reservoir," refilled each winter, then gradually emptying into streams, rivers, and groundwater basins. Every river canyon in California that is suitable for a major dam has been developed. Flowing rivers have been transformed into reservoirs; the water often now travels through irrigation ditches and city pipes, leaving some river channels dry. Plants and animals that are just as dependent on water must settle for whatever people are willing to share with them. The transformation of the state's water-dependent habitats is greatly responsible for the length of California's list of endangered and threatened species.

The first section in this book considers the water cycle that moves vital molecules of $H_2O$ across the California landscape, creating precipitation and climate patterns that shape the state's relationship with water. Next, the original waterscape of California is compared to today's scene, across 10 distinct hydrologic regions. In the third section, the distribution system that carries water between regions to serve human purposes is detailed. Many of the changes in the California waterscape followed the creation of the transport systems described here. The wide range of challenges that have resulted are described in the fourth section, a survey of environmental concerns, lost habitat, endangered species, pollution, domestic water quality issues, and of ties between water and growth. Finally, attention turns to ways of addressing these challenges to shape California's water future. Statewide planning, water marketing, recycling, desalination, conservation, and the future of dams in this state are some of the topics.

This book is a natural history guide, but one that recognizes the overwhelming role of humanity in the story of California water. The focus here is on a contemporary understanding of the natural waterscape and watersheds of the state and of the extended watersheds that people created by redirecting water across the West. The goal is to help Californians better appreciate the water that emerges from their taps, what it takes to move it there, and what changes occur in environments along the way.

Today, overall demand exceeds the supply of developed water in California. Understanding the natural role of water in this environment and the complexities of the interconnected water system is the first step toward wise choices by society's decision makers and by every Californian.

See how every raindrop and snowflake, every skyborne molecule of $H_2O$ that falls…is also a child of Ocean and Sun…. See how those streams and rivers, as Aldo Leopold pointed out, are "round," running past our feet and out to sea, then rising up in great tapestries of gravity-defying vapor to blow and flow back over us in oceans of cloud, fall once more upon the slopes as rain and snow, then congeal and start seaward, forming the perpetual prayer wheels we call watersheds.

—DAVID DUNCAN, *MY STORY AS TOLD BY WATER*

Especially as I drink the last of my water, I believe that we are subjects of the planet's hydrologic process, too proud to write ourselves into textbooks along with clouds, rivers, and morning dew.

—CRAIG CHILDS, *THE SECRET KNOWLEDGE OF WATER*

# A Great Water Wheel

A partnership between land and a planetary water cycle produces the California climate and shapes the natural landscape of the state. California's weather is generated primarily by westerly winds off the Pacific Ocean. In the winter, low pressure in the northern Pacific sends cold, wet storms to the state. California receives 75% of its annual precipitation between November and March, the majority from December through February. The dry weather of summer is associated with a high-pressure "dome" over the Pacific. Such "Mediterranean" climates, with wet winters and summer droughts, occur on the west coasts of continents in the middle latitudes due to global patterns of atmospheric pressure circulating over the oceans.

California's rainfall is heaviest in the north and decreases toward the south (map 1). Eureka, surrounded by redwood

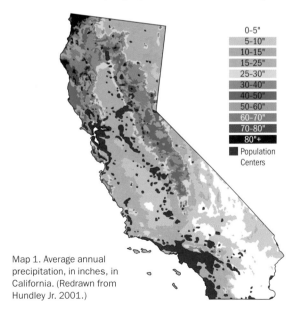

0-5"
5-10"
10-15"
15-25"
25-30"
30-40"
40-50"
50-60"
60-70"
70-80"
80"+
Population Centers

Map 1. Average annual precipitation, in inches, in California. (Redrawn from Hundley Jr. 2001.)

Plate 1. Mammoth Creek. Six months of winter snow and a brief summer growing season are one version of the California climate.

rain forests, usually receives more than 50 inches of rain each winter. That North Coast town has as much claim to a "California climate" as Los Angeles does, with only 15 inches on average. It *does* rain in Southern California, contrary to the myth popularized by real estate promoters and Hollywood, and Los Angeles does experience seasons. Winter rains activate the Southern California growing season, as dormant plants awake and seeds of annual plants germinate. Summer brings a seasonal drought, and the autumn transition includes hot, dry Santa Ana winds and wildfires. Mountain communities such as Lake Tahoe and Mammoth Lakes experience yet another version of California weather, with six months of winter snow and the brief summer growing season characteristic of alpine landscapes (pl. 1).

California's diverse landscape is responsible for this wide range of precipitation patterns. The state's coastline stretches 800 miles from Oregon to Mexico. A map of California, superimposed over the East Coast of the United States, would extend from southern Maine all the way to South Carolina,

Map 2. Landform provinces in California.
(Redrawn from Schoenherr 1992.)

crossing more than nine degrees of latitude. But California has more diverse weather and climate than the East, because its 100 million acres contain the tallest mountain ranges in the 48 contiguous states and desert basins that lie hundreds of feet below sea level (map 2).

Rainfall and snowfall result when humid air masses blow in from the ocean and interact with the state's mountain ranges. Moist air, moved inland by the prevailing westerlies, pushes up against California's mountain backbones, which

Plate 2. Air cooling and condensing as mountains push it up.

wring vapor out of air as it rises, cools, and condenses (pl. 2). Precipitation generally increases two to four inches for each 300-foot rise. Seasonal snowfall totals about two feet at the 3,000-foot elevation in the Sierra Nevada foothills, but increases to 34 feet on Donner Summit, the famous 7,000-foot pass where the Donner party spent a tragic winter. The Sierra Nevada occupies one-fifth of the land area of California and has a major influence on the climate, weather, and water supply of much of the state. Its crest extends 430 miles; 8,000-foot summits in the north rise to over 14,000 feet in the south, intercepting the westerly jet stream at higher and higher elevations. Most of the precipitation in the Sierra Nevada falls as winter snow (pl. 3). In Plumas County, north of Lake Tahoe, an average of 90 inches of precipitation falls at 5,000 feet. The same elevation in the southern Sierra receives as little as 30 inches.

Plate 3. Sierra Nevada precipitation in the form of winter snow.

As air descends the east side of California's mountain ranges, the process is reversed. Air becomes warmer and holds more water vapor. Relatively dry "rain shadows" are the result. The Sierra Nevada rain shadow created the Great Basin desert. The Coast Ranges produce a rain-shadow effect for the Central Valley, although a major gap at San Francisco Bay lets more moisture directly strike the northern Sierra Nevada. The Mojave and Colorado Deserts lie in the rain shadow of the southern Sierra Nevada but are primarily influenced by

Plate 4. The Mojave Desert in the rain shadow of the Sierra Nevada.

the Transverse and Peninsular Ranges. The Mojave Desert town of Barstow averages only four inches of rain per year; Imperial, farther south in the Colorado Desert, is even drier. (Pl. 4.)

A broad cross section through the state, beginning near San Luis Obispo and extending roughly northeastward, intersecting the mountain ranges at right angles, would pass through the Central Valley near Visalia, cross Sequoia National Park, and take in the Owens Valley town of Independence. San Luis Obispo, at the base of low mountains in the Coast Ranges, averages 22 inches of rain; Coalinga, in the Coast Ranges' rain shadow and down on the floor of the Central Valley, receives only seven inches. Farther east, just below the Sierra Nevada foothills, Visalia picks up 11 inches. Giant Forest, in Sequoia National Park, is at 7,000 feet; snow and rain there total 46 inches of precipitation (pl. 5). Independence is in a desert created by the Sierra's rain shadow and averages only five inches of rain. East of the White Mountains, in Death Valley, 178 feet below sea level, annual precipitation is a mere two inches at Greenland Ranch (Fig. 1.)

California receives almost 200 million acre-feet of precip-

Plate 5. Snow at 7,000 feet in Sequoia National Park.

itation in an average year. (One acre-foot equals 325,851 gallons, which would cover a football field one foot deep. Planners commonly figure that one acre-foot serves the annual domestic needs of one to two families, or five to eight people, depending on how wisely it is used and conserved.) Water that falls on the state may evaporate back into the atmosphere, be used by plants that then return vapor to the air, or soak deep into groundwater basins. What remains is about 71 million acre-feet of "runoff" water, which moves across the landscape and is the water most accessible to people. Streams draining the sodden North Coast contain about 40 percent of this runoff. The Sacramento River basin generates another 31 percent, mostly originating with the Sierra Nevada snowpack. Snowmelt from the southern Sierra drains into the San Joaquin and Tulare Valleys, producing much of the balance. (Map 3.) The Colorado River receives almost no runoff originating inside California, but because it serves as the state's southeastern border, California receives 4.4 million acre-feet from it. This apportionment, along with Klamath River water out of Oregon, allows water planners to figure on a statewide supply of 78 million acre-feet of annual runoff.

The Sierra Nevada snowpack peaks by April 1 and then begins melting. By midsummer it is gone, except for a few small glaciers and snowfields on north-facing exposures that are shaded from direct sunlight. The delayed release of snowpack water overlaps only partly with the optimum growing season for plants in California. Moisture is most available in the winter, when temperatures are low, and is scarce during the long, warm days that optimize growth. Urban and agricultural water demands are out of sync with the natural runoff pattern, at their peak during summer and their low point during winter. California's natural vegetation evolved adaptations to

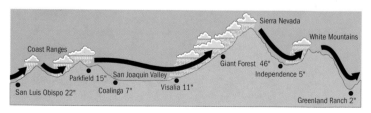

Fig.1. Influence of topography on precipitation; a southwest-northeast cross section of California. (Redrawn from Durrenberger 1968.)

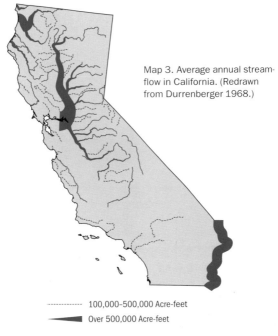

Map 3. Average annual stream-flow in California. (Redrawn from Durrenberger 1968.)

------------- 100,000–500,000 Acre-feet
▬▬▬▬ Over 500,000 Acre-feet

the local patterns. Many annual plants flower quickly in spring and produce seeds that sleep through the long drought of summer and early autumn. Winter rains break that dormancy. Some perennial shrubs and trees rely on deep root systems to tap water even during the long seasonal droughts. Others go dormant, simply shutting down their metabolisms. Riparian vegetation found along riverbanks and in wetlands benefits from year-round water availability. The New England pattern of four seasons—lush, green springs; hot, wet summers that encourage plant growth; autumn color before leaves are dropped; and freezing winter weather— is found in California only in mountain and foothill river canyons. There plants can keep their roots wet, and local hydrologic conditions mimic the New England pattern (pl. 6).

Water moving within California is part of a greater plane-

Plate 6. Plants watered year-round by a mountain creek.

tary water cycle that includes many circular movements, wheels within wheels (fig. 2). Water is continuously shifting among three "reservoirs": the ocean, the atmosphere, and the land. These are connected by precipitation, evaporation, and plant absorption and transpiration (evaporation through leaf pores). Water is perpetually changing form and traveling the globe. It has been said that we drink the same water the dinosaurs drank. That is not entirely accurate for specific water molecules. During photosynthesis, for example, these molecules split into oxygen and hydrogen atoms. Yet it is true that no water is lost in the overall planetary balance; water returns. The respiration of plants and animals recycles it, reversing the photosynthesis equation by consuming oxygen while breaking complex molecules into water and carbon dioxide. Fire, an important decomposition agent in the natural California landscape, produces the same results. And when organisms die and decompose, water is reconstituted.

This planetary recycling is powered by the sun, which evaporates water from the ocean and the land. In photosynthesis, the sun's energy is also what splits the bonds holding water molecules together. Of the water vapor returned to the atmosphere, 16 percent comes from transpiration by land plants (pl. 7); most of the rest comes from the ocean. At any given moment only a thousandth of one percent (.00001) of the planet's total water is in the air. Yet that small percentage produces thick coastal fogs, dramatic thunderheads, and drenching downpours. In a journal entry written during a January storm, John Muir marveled "that so much rain can be stored in the sky" ([1938] 1979, 335). The recycling that replenishes atmospheric vapor is so constant and voluminous

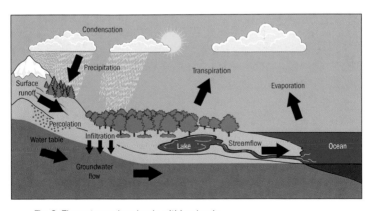

Fig. 2. The water cycle: wheels within wheels.

Plate 7. Evap-
otranspiration
returning
water to the
atmosphere.

that this water is completely replaced every eight days and the equivalent of all the oceans' water passes through the atmosphere every 3,100 years.

Two-thirds of the Earth's surface is covered by liquid water. Philip Ball wrote, in *Life's Matrix: A Biography of Water* (2001, 22), "We call our home Earth—but Water would be more apt." Over 97 percent is salt water, though, and over two-thirds of the freshwater is locked up in ice caps and glaciers. Less than one percent of the total is available freshwater, and most of that is belowground, in aquifers that are never fully accessible. On this watery planet, just .016 percent (.00016) of the precious fluid is "active" freshwater, moving through lakes, rivers, the atmosphere, and living creatures. (Fig. 3.)

The cogs in the water-recycling wheel revolve at different speeds, like different-sized gears meshing inside an enormously complex clock. Vapor evaporated from the surface of the sea may circulate for only a few hours or for days. Deep-ocean water may take thousands of years to complete a circuit of evaporation, condensation, and return. Some of the water in the polar ice caps may remain solid for millions of years. The ice in some small Sierra Nevada glaciers has been there for nearly a thousand years. Under certain conditions, groundwater can be trapped in deep, confined aquifers, held back from the water cycle for thousands of years. At its own speed, however, groundwater does participate in the cycle. It feeds springs, rivers, or lakes, and it is replenished when surface water percolates into the ground.

Water may travel for weeks through California's river arteries before finally returning to the sea or ending its journey in inland waters such as Mono Lake. Almost anywhere along these routes it may be shunted aside, pulled in by the roots of a plant or drunk by an animal.

Water is essential for life on Earth and is the critical habitat factor that shapes California's ecosystems. As the leaf and root

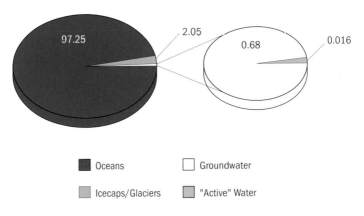

Fig. 3. Planetary water reservoirs (percent of planetary water).

Plate 8. Needles and leaves designed to conserve water.

designs of plants adapt to climate, elevation, soil, and topography, both the gathering and the conservation of water are of supreme importance. Bands of different flowers lining a vernal pool sort themselves out by their particular relationships with water. The spiny leaves of a Joshua tree *(Yucca brevifolia engelmann)*, like the extremely efficient kidneys of a kangaroo rat, are water-conservation adaptations to life in the desert. (Pl. 8.) Indeed, everywhere in the state—in the wetland marshes rimming San Francisco Bay, the grassy prairies of the Central Valley, the North Coast rain forests, the chaparral shrublands of Southern California, the foothill oak woodlands, and the pine forests of the Sierra Nevada—all forms of life accommodate to the local availability of water. Photosynthesis requires water, often in enormous amounts. Plants combine water with carbon dioxide to manufacture food for themselves and the herbivores that feed on them; in the process, they replenish the atmosphere with oxygen gas.

Various mechanisms and behaviors foster "best management practices" for water conservation by living things. At the boundaries between multicellular bodies and the rest of the world, barriers of skin, bark, scales, or mucous membranes regulate water passage in and out. Every living cell has a membrane that encloses and regulates its internal concoction of water and essential chemicals. Multicellular organisms bathe their cells in watery environments. Water management is critical to homeostasis, the maintenance of the internal conditions necessary for life.

*We* are bodies of water. Humans can live without food for weeks, but die within days when deprived of water. Our bodies are 65 percent water (our brains more than 95 percent); a 150-pound human body contains over 12 gallons of water. We need to replenish about two and a half quarts a day, one-third from drinking and the rest in foods, as we lose water in breath, sweat, and urine. Water is the primary medium for biochemical reactions and a participant in many of the essential processes of life. It helps break down our food, then carries the digestion products to our cells. It regulates temperature and transports dissolved oxygen and carbon dioxide through our circulatory systems. Proteins that rely partly on their shapes to fulfill their jobs as enzymes are folded into those shapes by bonds with water in the fluid of our cells. As cellular metabolism generates wastes, water dissolves them and moves them across filtration membranes in our kidneys, returning them (and the water itself) to the environment.

Water is so essential to us that it is amazing we ever take it for granted. If it is our most precious resource, that is not simply because the supply sometimes grows scarce. $H_2O$ is the vital essence of life on Earth, an almost magical molecule. A full appreciation of our relationship with California water begins at the molecular level.

## The Vital Molecule

Water is so familiar that we seldom give any thought to what sets this particular molecule apart from other substances commonly found in our lives. Unusual characteristics are behind water's critical importance. "Water is life's true and unique medium," Philip Ball has written. "That the only solvent with the refinement needed for nature's most intimate machinations happens to be the one that covers two-thirds of our planet is surely something to take away and marvel at" (2001, 268).

Most solids, liquids, or gases that we encounter naturally are found in just one phase. Minerals, such as silica or calcium carbonate, that form rocks and soils remain solid (unless heated to extremes by volcanic action or movement of the plates that form the Earth's crust). Other elements and compounds, too, stay in a single phase under normal circumstances. "Silicon vapor" is not part of our daily experience or vocabulary. Neither is "liquid wood" or, for that matter, "solid air." Decomposition or digestion breaks molecules apart to build something new, but this is not simply a matter of phase changes. The water molecule, however, is widely abundant on this planet in all three phases: as solid ice, liquid water, and gaseous water vapor (pl. 9). When most other molecules *are* transformed, those changes regularly involve water because it is so nearly ubiquitous, dissolves most anything, and is good at carrying other materials along with it.

The explanation for water's unusual phase character also helps explain why water contains "an invisible flame…that creates not heat but life," as described by David Duncan in *My Story As Told By Water* (2001, 190). Water is a "community

Plate 9. Ice crystals, one widely abundant form of water.

molecule." That is, water molecules constantly form, break, and re-form bonds with one another. Those bonds produce a cohesive tendency that is behind most of water's special attributes. Working together, $H_2O$ molecules pick up the colors of the sky, create the pleasing sounds of water and gravity working together, and shape our most beautiful landscapes.

The cohesiveness is explained by the relationship between two hydrogen atoms and one oxygen atom. H-O-H is a polar molecule, more positively charged at the hydrogen ends and more negatively charged toward the oxygen atom. Because opposite charges attract, hydrogen within one water molecule will orient toward the oxygen in another. Each $H_2O$ molecule can form such "hydrogen bonds" with up to four others (fig. 4).

This bonding explains many unique properties. $H_2O$'s po-

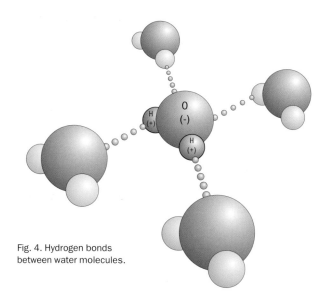

Fig. 4. Hydrogen bonds
between water molecules.

larity makes it the "universal solvent" because its charged ends
seek out opposite charges on many other kinds of molecules
as well. Water weasels its way between such molecules, sepa-
rating them and carrying them into solution. It dissolves so
many things that truly pure water is rarely, if ever, found in
nature. The chemistry of your local water supply reflects
whatever rock and soil it has touched. Even atmospheric
vapor, distilled to purity by evaporation, soon finds substances to react with in the air. Acid rain is one familiar and
unpleasant result.

Bonded cohesiveness also accounts for the ability of California's 300-foot-tall redwood trees to lift water from the
ground up to their topmost branches inside cellular tubes—
water ropes that move against gravity because tension is applied from the top, where leaves pass water out to the atmosphere. It also explains the surface tension that allows a water
strider to skate across the surface of a pond (pl. 10).

Unlike almost every other liquid naturally found on Earth,

Plate 10. A water strider on the surface of a pond, skating on the surface tension created by water molecules.

water expands when it freezes. The expansion begins, oddly, *before* the freezing point is reached. As cooling water drops below 40 degrees F, it suddenly becomes less dense—the opposite of its behavior above that temperature. It takes on a regular crystalline shape with empty space between the oppositely charged hydrogen and oxygen portions of neighboring molecules. Because of this strange behavior, solid water— ice—is less dense than liquid water, and ice floats (pl. 11). If the water in mountain lakes behaved like most liquids, cooling at the surface would cause denser ice to settle to the bottom, and gradually the lake would freeze solid right up to the surface. Because ice floats, fish and other aquatic creatures can carry on through the winter beneath insulating ice layers that eventually arrest further cooling of the depths. Because water expands when it freezes, mountain residents have to protect pipes from bursting in the winter. The internal liquid environment in all living things must also be protected from freeze-expansion that could destroy cellular membranes and tissues. Freezing water even shapes the California landscape wherever water in cracks expands as ice, causing rock to peel and break.

Plate 11. Ice floating on a mountain lake.

The cohesiveness of hydrogen bonds means that it requires an unusual amount of energy for water to change phases. Water has high melting and boiling points because bonded molecules resist being pulled apart. Thus, for example, when sweat evaporates, a great deal of heat is carried off, efficiently cooling our bodies. Water also resists too-rapid heating. It takes more heat to raise the temperature of water than to raise that of most other liquid or solid substances by the same amount. Though a sandy beach in the sun gets very hot, the nearby seawater or a lawn bordering the beach remains cool. Both the ocean and the grass heat up slowly and are constantly losing energy through evaporation.

The cohesive attraction between molecules of water also means that there is a direct connection between you and your watershed, through hundreds of miles of pipes, treatment plants, aqueducts, reservoirs, and rivers. Continuous "ropes" of water may extend from a San Diego faucet all the way to the northern Sierra Nevada and the Colorado Rockies. "Pull" from your end and water molecules transmit that tiny force, reacting all the way up the line.

# "Normal" Weather: Anything but "Average"

> And it never failed that during the dry years the people forgot about the rich years, and during the wet years they lost all memory of the dry years. It was always that way.
>
> —JOHN STEINBECK, *EAST OF EDEN*

The normal climate of California includes droughts and years that are particularly wet (pl. 12). Very rarely does California weather actually match long-term averages. The state's average annual runoff totals 71 million acre-feet, but the range is tremendous—as little as 15 million acre-feet during the severe drought year of 1977, but up to 135 million acre-feet in the exceptionally wet winter of 1983. The annual volume in Sierra Nevada rivers can be 20 times as great in very wet years as in very dry years (fig. 5).

Such year-to-year variations are partially tied to the variable Pacific Ocean temperatures collectively known as the El Niño Southern Oscillation. When warmer currents shift eastward in the Pacific, toward the coasts of North and South America, winters are wetter than normal, though their severity varies considerably. El Niño events are interspersed with La Niña events, with colder-than-normal ocean temperatures and, usually, below-normal precipitation.

## Droughts

No simple criteria define a drought. Water providers in California may announce a drought emergency whenever there is too little supply to meet demand. Different regions may per-

Plate 12. A sign of drought, part of the normal weather cycle in California.

ceive a given year's rainfall totals differently, depending on their local storage capacities, alternative supply sources, and regional populations. The most severe recorded California drought occurred from 1929 to 1934. It set the standard that has been applied ever since for developing needed reservoir storage capacity in the state's water system. The driest

Plate 13. A boat ramp at Courtright Reservoir, in the Sierra National Forest, stranded by drought in 2002.

Plate 14. A snow survey site in the Sierra Nevada.

recorded water year spanned the winter of 1976 to 1977; state-wide runoff was only 21 percent of average. That extremely severe condition lasted only one year. The drought of 1987 to 1993 was a close match to the drought of 1929 to 1934 in both length and severity (table 1).

With such variability between seasons and between years, water storage systems, particularly reservoirs created by dams, have become important tools in moderating the swings in water supply. (Pl. 13.) The Sierra Nevada snowpack is our largest and most effective "reservoir" (pl. 14), slowly releasing its water in spring and summer. A storm that drops one inch

TABLE 1. Severity of extreme droughts in the Sacramento and San Joaquin Valleys

| | Sacramento Valley Runoff | | San Joaquin Valley Runoff | |
|---|---|---|---|---|
| | MAF/yr | % of Avg | MAF/yr | % of Avg |
| **1929–34** | 9.8 | 55% | 3.3 | 57% |
| **1976–77** | 6.6 | 37% | 1.5 | 26% |
| **1987–92** | 10.0 | 56% | 2.8 | 47% |

Source: California Department of Water Resources, 1998.

of rain in the lowlands may leave 10 inches of snow around the 5,000-foot elevation. The amount of water in the snowpack is not simply a product of snow depth. Snow that falls when it is cold often has less water content: one cubic foot of the powdery snow that falls at 14 degrees F may only produce .05 cubic foot of water, but at 32 degrees, a cubic foot of snow may contain four times as much.

In 1929, the state legislature established a statewide California Cooperative Snow Surveys Program, coordinated by the Department of Water Resources (DWR). State, national, and private agencies pool data from about 300 snow survey sites sampled each winter (pl. 15). The snowpack data, along with precipitation records, help DWR water planners forecast the water supply that will be available each spring and summer.

Though accurate rainfall and snowpack records only go back a century, dendrochronologists studying the thickness of annual tree rings can identify major historic weather patterns. Near San Diego, 560 years of tree rings were studied in bigcone spruce *(Pseudotsuga macrocarpa)*. Dry cycles averaging 15 years were found to be interspersed with wet cycles about 12 years long. A 420-year reconstruction of Sacramento River runoff data, also based upon tree rings, was used to establish the drought of 1929 to 1934 as the most severe in those four centuries.

Age dating of tree stumps that are now submerged in lakes and rivers has identified two epic drought periods in Califor-

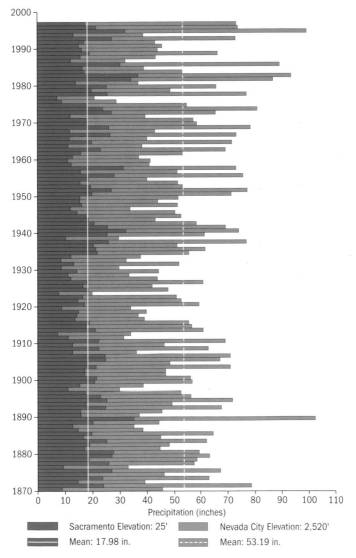

Fig. 5. Annual precipitation variability in the Central Valley watershed, 1870 to 1997. (Redrawn from Bay Institute of San Francisco 1998.)

Plate 15. The Sierra Nevada snowpack on May 23, 2002.

nia during the Middle Ages. Stumps at Mono Lake, Lake Tenaya, and Walker River show two medieval droughts, one lasting 140 years and the other at least 100 years. The twentieth century was not "normal" when compared to this longer record; it was, in fact, California's third- or fourth-wettest century of the past 4,000 years. Scott Stine, in his report on this research, noted, "Since statehood, Californians have been living in the best of climatic times. And we've taken advantage of these best of times by building the most colossal urban and agricultural infrastructure in the entire world, all dependent on huge amounts of water, and all based on the assumption that runoff from the Sierra Nevada will continue as it has during the past 150 years" (1994, 548).

# Floods

At the other extreme, floods are equally normal products of the California climate. The Central Valley used to flood annually, becoming a great inland sea when the Sacramento and San Joaquin Rivers, carrying snowmelt from the Sierra Nevada, left their banks to reinhabit the floodplain of the valley floor. Fertile sediments deposited on that flat land were attractive to farmers. Once modern human settlements were established, attempts began to straitjacket the rivers with levees and dikes. Riparian forests were cut down so crops could be planted right up to the edges of the rivers. Towns also were planted, and some grew into major cities. Sacramento, the state's capital, is at the confluence of the American and Sacramento Rivers. "River City" has a long history of floods, and concern about levees and upstream dams remains an issue today. For cities located on floodplains around the state, dams and levees built to prevent floods have often only postponed them. (Pl. 16.) When warm winter rain events, dubbed the "Pineapple Express," fall onto snow deposited earlier in the winter, rivers suddenly swell. Water planners and engineers established the "100-year flood" concept not to indicate the actual frequency of such events, but to predict the likelihood of serious floods. Unfortunately, such predictions were based only on the records of flooding available since statehood, in 1850.

California experienced major floods in 1850, 1862, 1955, 1964, 1995, and 1997. The January 1997 event was the largest flood disaster in the state's history (defined by damage to human structures, rather than quantity of runoff water flowing over floodplains). That year 120,000 people were forced from homes and 300 square miles of agricultural land were flooded (pl. 17). Ironically, that flood was followed by a

Plate 16. Trailer park flooded by the San Joaquin River in 1997.

Plate 17. Evacuation during a 1972 flood.

record-setting dry period from February through June 1997. Flooding in 1986 had also marked the beginning of a severe multiyear drought. Those kinds of events make managing for flood protection a challenging trick, one that often conflicts with the maximum storage of water for later use. If water is released during the winter to make room for spring floodwater, the result can be less summer storage.

During the 1990s, extreme precipitation events in California increased by 20 percent. That may be a consequence of global warming, which is expected to produce wetter and warmer winter storms.

Despite our efforts to control such episodes, high runoff and flooding have played an important role in natural water cycling in California, fertilizing floodplains and helping to shape the landscape. Water in motion, whether liquid or frozen, also has the power to transform landforms. Glaciers carved broad, U-shaped valleys, such as Hetch Hetchy and Yosemite (pl. 18). Rivers incised narrower, V-shaped canyons, such as the American River canyon in the Sierra Nevada foothills (pl. 19). They also carried debris sediments on down to the Central Valley, building its rich alluvial soils.

Plate 18. U-shaped granite basins scoured by glaciers where the Merced River drops over Nevada and Vernal Falls in Yosemite National Park.

Plate 19. A V-shaped canyon gradually cut by liquid water along the east fork of the Carson River.

John Muir listened to the voices of water as it did such work, and wrote of "silvery branches interlacing on a thousand mountains, singing their way home to the sea," or "booming in falls, gliding, glancing with cool soothing, murmuring" (1901, 181, 182) (pl. 20). Mountain streams, Muir said, sang "the history of every avalanche or earthquake and of snow, all easily recognized by the human ear...beside a thousand other facts so small and spoken by the stream in so low a voice the human ear cannot hear them" ([1938] 1979, 95) (pl. 21).

Wherever rain falls from the sky over California and rivers sing of their interactions with the land, water speaks in eloquent voices across this state's water landscape.

Plate 20.
Mill Creek
in Lundy
Canyon.

Plate 21. The voice of water.

*By such a river it is impossible to believe that one will ever be tired or old. Every sense applauds it. Taste it, feel its chill on the teeth: it is purity absolute. And listen again to its sounds: get far enough away so that the noise of falling tons of water does not stun the ears, and hear how much is going on underneath—a whole symphony of smaller sounds, hiss and splash and gurgle, the small talk of side channels, the whisper of blown and scattered spray gathering itself and beginning to flow again, secret and irresistible, among the wet rocks.*

—WALLACE STEGNER, *SOUND OF MOUNTAIN WATER*

# Pristine Waterscape

Study a map of California's pristine waterscape (map 4). Some of its major features are startlingly unfamiliar to twenty-first-century Californians. The massive Tulare Lake, far bigger than Lake Tahoe, occupies the southern end of the Central Valley. Farther south are the smaller Buena Vista and Kern Lakes. Those three lakes, gone from most of today's maps, are connected by expanses of freshwater marsh, sloughs that flood during wet seasons. The Salton Sea is missing; its basin is marked as a region of saline land that experiences "intermittent water." (At least four times between 700 and 1580 A.D., sediments built up until the Colorado River jumped from its channel and flooded the Salton Sink, creating lakes that gradually evaporated after the river shifted back toward its other terminus in the Gulf of California.) Owens Lake *does* have water—a blue expanse that would be refreshing for contemporary travelers in the Eastern Sierra who pass by the dry, dusty lakebed. It too would spread over nearby lands during wet cycles. (Mapmakers estimate "natural shorelines," but the surface area of many lakes fluctuated tremendously with California's natural climate variations.) In the northeast corner of the state, Lower Klamath, Tule, and Goose Lakes appear much larger than they would on contemporary maps. All the state's rivers are free flowing, of course, so the map does not show reservoirs later created by dams. A modern map at this scale would show hundreds of these; one at a larger scale would show thousands.

Two of our major river arteries—the Sacramento and San Joaquin Rivers—gather water from tributaries that drain 37 percent of the state. They merge into a complex of estuary channels that pass water through San Francisco Bay into the Pacific Ocean. Though contemporary maps typically show rivers as solid blue lines following these historic routes, today some stretches have been completely dewatered. For example, since Friant Dam was built in the 1940s, almost no San Joa-

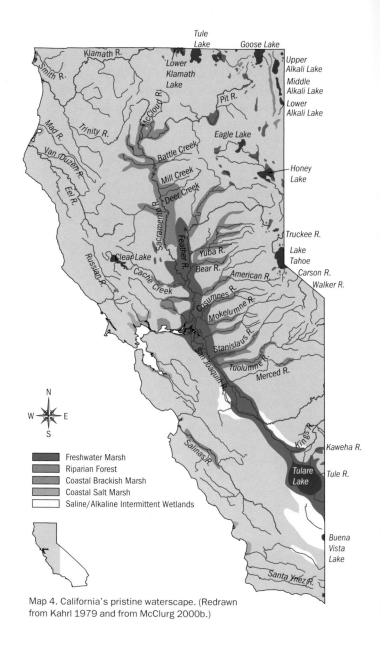

Map 4. California's pristine waterscape. (Redrawn from Kahrl 1979 and from McClurg 2000b.)

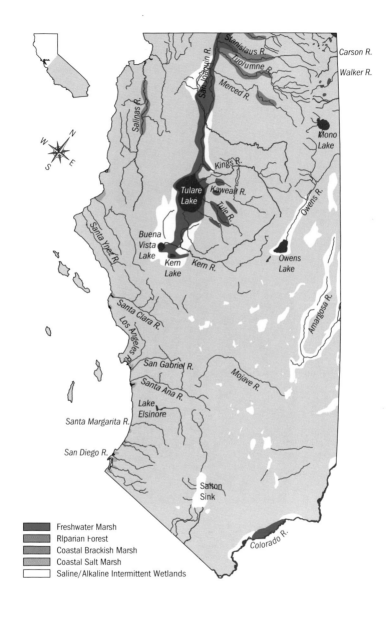

Carson R.

Walker R.

Stanislaus R.

Tuolumne R.

San Joaquin R.

Merced R.

Salinas R.

Mono Lake

Kings R.

Kaweah R.

Tulare Lake

Tule R.

Owens R.

Buena Vista Lake

Kern Lake

Kern R.

Owens Lake

Santa Ynez R.

Amargosa R.

Santa Clara R.

Los Angeles R.

San Gabriel R.

Mojave R.

Santa Ana R.

Lake Elsinore

Santa Margarita R.

San Diego R.

Salton Sink

Colorado R.

- Freshwater Marsh
- Riparian Forest
- Coastal Brackish Marsh
- Coastal Salt Marsh
- Saline/Alkaline Intermittent Wetlands

quin River water has come down as far as the Delta. About 60 miles of its channel are dry, the flow diverted to irrigation. Every river in the arid Tulare Lake basin has dry portions due to diversions into irrigation channels and aqueducts.

Besides the unfamiliar lakes and rivers, the most eye-catching features on the map of the pristine waterscape are more than five million acres of wetlands. Four million of those acres, including both freshwater marsh and riparian forest, sprawl the length of the Central Valley. They do not just parallel rivers, but spread across much of the valley floor. That reflects the winter and spring flooding that once regularly turned the basin (where much of the land is near sea level) into a vast sea, slowly draining back into the rivers. Today only 350,000 acres of the valley's marshes remain, and nine of every 10 acres of its riparian woodlands are also gone. Water that en-

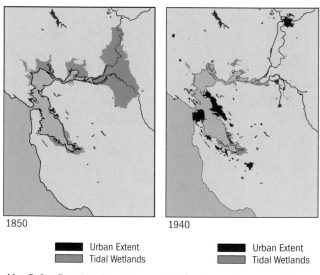

1850

■ Urban Extent
■ Tidal Wetlands

Map 5. San Francisco Bay–Delta wetlands and urbanization, 1850. (Redrawn from U.S. Geological Survey, no date.)

1940

■ Urban Extent
■ Tidal Wetlands

Map 6. San Francisco Bay–Delta wetlands and urbanization, 1940. (Redrawn from U.S. Geological Survey, no date.)

ters most of the remaining wetlands is artificially managed, and natural flooding is a rare reminder that the forces that formed the California waterscape refuse to be fully tamed.

Less obvious on the map, yet totaling hundreds of thousands of acres, marshes also border much of the coastline at the mouths of rivers and around bays and lagoons in both Northern and Southern California. An extensive freshwater marsh stands out along the west bank of the Colorado River, in striking contrast to the neighboring desert. San Francisco Bay is surrounded by 200,000 acres of brackish and salt marshes. (Only 35,000 acres still survive today. The surface of the bay itself has also shrunk by 240 square miles as open water has succumbed to urban landfills [maps 5–7].) Another 80,000 acres of marshland border Suisun Bay, where water emerges from the maze of Delta channels and is passed along

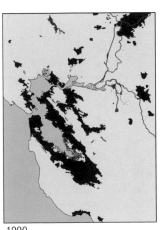

to San Pablo Bay and San Francisco Bay. Today, what remains of Suisun Marsh is still the largest salt marsh in the lower 48 states, representing 12 percent of the total wetlands acreage left in California.

1990

Urban Extent
Tidal Wetlands

Map 7. San Francisco Bay–Delta wetlands and Urbanization, 1990. (Redrawn from U.S. Geological Survey, no date.)

Plate 22. Sacramento–San Joaquin Delta channels and islands.

The Delta, where water spreads into 700 miles of channels, forms the largest estuary on the West Coast. It once supported 345,000 acres of tidal marsh but is now down to 8,000 acres. Nearly all Delta marshlands have been transformed into islands surrounded by levees (pl. 22). Most of the farmland behind those levees sits below sea level. When peat soils typical of the Delta were "reclaimed," they became dry and light enough to be carried off by the winds that funnel through the gap in the Coast Ranges. The winds carry away as much as two inches a year of Delta peat, and the islands keep on sinking, protected only by the levees.

Freshwater that flows into the sea acts as a hydraulic dam that holds back salt water. The distance that salt water moves inland with each rising tide is thus determined by the amount of runoff coming through the Delta and into the bay. The mixing of the waters determines habitat quality for resident fish, such as Delta Smelt *(Hypomesus transpacificus)* and Sacramento Splittail *(Pogonichthys macrolepidotus)*, and for anadromous fish, such as salmon, Steelhead Trout *(Oncorhynchus mykiss)*, and Pacific Lamprey *(Entosphenus tridentatus)*, which travel between inland spawning sites and the sea.

Plate 23. Upper Newport Harbor, one of the remnant coastal marshes of Southern California.

Historically, during particularly high flow periods, the bay could become mostly fresh. During droughts, salt water could move all the way through the Delta to the river mouths.

Only about half of the river water that historically moved from the Delta out to sea normally makes it that far today. About seven million acre-feet of the freshwater reaching the estuary are pumped from there into aqueducts and shipped south. The Delta has become the diversion point for water serving two-thirds of California's population and irrigating San Joaquin Valley and Tulare Basin farms. As a result, salinity is higher in the bay, and the zone where salt and freshwater mix has shifted inland.

Southern California wetlands have also declined or disappeared. Sportsman and author Charles Holder described Southern California coastal marshes, as he knew them in 1906, in his book *Life in the Open* (51–52): "All the country to the south of the Palos Verde, near San Pedro, and extending to Long Beach, is a shallow back bay, a series of lagunas or canals, often running back into the country to form some little pond or lake. At Alamitos, where the San Gabriel River reaches the sea, and at Balsa Chica...and other places along shore to San Diego we shall find these lagunas, or sea swamps, the home of

the duck, goose, and swan. The season begins in November…
the air is clear, and the distant mountains stand out with mar-
velous distinctness…. No more beautiful sight than this can
be seen in Southern California when these vast flocks pass up
and down, silhouetted against the chaparral of the mountain
slopes."

Ninety percent of the coastal marsh acreage from Morro
Bay to San Diego is gone. Southern Californians can find
remnants of it at increasingly rare places, such as Seal Beach
and Upper Newport Bay in Orange County, San Diego Bay,
and the Tijuana Estuary (pl. 23).

The marshlands that persist are vitally important for
many plants, fish, mammals, and breeding and migratory
birds. The nutrient mix in coastal estuaries makes them 10
times as productive as the open ocean. Salt marshes serve as
nurseries for the majority of oceanic fish and shellfish that are
commercially harvested. Fifty percent of the animals listed as
endangered or threatened in the United States utilize wetland
habitats. Wetlands serve as natural places for floodwaters to
spread. Their vegetation controls erosion and cleans water by
trapping and filtering sediments.

Wildlife once found in California's marshlands included a
half million Tule Elk *(Cervus elaphus nannodes)*, enough
Beaver *(Castor canadensis)* to attract trappers long before
statehood, and even Grizzly Bears *(Ursus arctos)*, so ubiquitous in the lowlands of California that they became the sym-
bol of the state. Enormous numbers of migrating waterfowl
took advantage of the state's wetlands each spring and fall.
Sixty million ducks and geese still used Central Valley wetlands in 1950, but by 1996, only three million of the birds
traveling the Pacific Flyway found refuge in the remnant valley marshes. (Pl. 24.)

A unique type of wetlands habitat, the vernal pool, was
once found on millions of acres in the Central Valley, in Sierra
Nevada foothills, in Coast Range valleys, and along the South
Coast basins. A vernal pool is a tiny watershed, an ephemeral

Plate 24. Waterfowl at the Modoc National Wildlife Refuge.

ecological island, where water collects during the wet season over impermeable hardpan or rock. During the summer such pools dry up, but tiny cysts and seeds lie dormant in the bottom mud, waiting for another wet cycle. Winter rains awaken fairy shrimp, Tadpole Shrimp *(Lepidurus packardi),* insects, and plants that are specially adapted to and completely dependent on these environments. Through the spring, as the ponds gradually shrink, rainbow bands of flowers ring them, segregated by the particular water requirements of each species (pl. 25). Those that need to keep their roots constantly wet grow and bloom closest to the diminishing water body. Farther out are those that prefer drier conditions. Before a pool completely dries, life cycles are rapidly completed. Encysted eggs and seeds settle once again to the bottom mud.

Vernal pools range in size from the 180-acre Table Mountain Lake in Tehama County down to small "hog wallows." About 90 percent of the Central Valley's vernal pools have been lost to plowing and leveling by farmers or to concrete and asphalt. California's list of endangered or threatened species includes five species of fairy shrimp and a tadpole shrimp indigenous to vernal pools. Much of the remaining

Plate 25. A vernal pool, with flowers sorted by their particular needs for water.

vernal-pool habitat coexists with cattle ranching along the rim of the Great Valley. The protection of vernal pools became an issue when the University of California began planning its newest campus near Merced on land containing 20,000 acres of the now-rare habitat.

The 20,000 miles of rivers and streams in California form 60 major watersheds. Today only one of the state's major river systems, the Smith River on the North Coast, is completely free of dams. The Cosumnes River, in the central Sierra Nevada, is the only major drainage on the west side of the range that still has unregulated flow. Even the Cosumnes has minor dams that pool some of its water to serve diversion intakes (without interrupting all the flow or blocking fish migration).

Eighty California river segments that retain their primitive character have been added to the federal Wild and Scenic Rivers system. Those segments, totaling 1,900 miles, are protected from dam construction and have management plans to guide activities along their corridors. "Wild" rivers "represent vestiges of primitive America"; this formal designation is akin to "wilderness" status. "Scenic" rivers have shorelines that are

Smith R.

Kalmath R.

Van Duzen R.

Trinity R.

Eel
R.

Feather R.,
Middle Fork

American R., North Fork

American R.,
Lower

Carson R., East Fork
West Walker R.

Tuolumne R.

Merced R.

Big Sur R.

Kings R.

Kern R.

Sisquoc R.

Sespe Creek

■ Federal and State Designation
■ State Designation Only
■ Federal Designation Only

Map 8. Wild and Scenic Rivers of California. (Redrawn from
California Department of Water Resources 1998.)

mostly primitive and undeveloped. "Recreational" status is given to areas easily accessible by roads and with some development. California's own state Wild and Scenic Rivers system prohibited damming and diversion of water and protected the first line of vegetation along rivers. All of California's designated rivers have been incorporated into the federal system (map 8).

## Groundwater

We naturally focus most on what we can see, but groundwater is seldom truly separate from surface water. It is another part of the natural water cycle, even if water travels very slowly through some groundwater basins. In an aquifer, or water-bearing layer, pores between particles of soil or rock are satu-

Plate 26.
Irrigation with
groundwater.

rated with water. The top of the saturated region is termed the "water table." Marshes or springs may occur where the water table either intersects the surface or finds a route through rock and is forced up by pressure from below. California's valley floors once had many artesian wells where such free-flowing springs reached the surface.

Groundwater is an important part of California's water supply. If you live in Norco or Visalia, Woodland or Mono City, you are among the Californians—more than one in four—who rely entirely upon groundwater. Half of California residents receive some groundwater through their faucets. About 760,000 acres of farmland are irrigated, in part, with groundwater (pl. 26). Forty percent of the state's average annual water supply comes from wells. That proportion can jump to 60 percent during severe drought years.

California has 450 known groundwater basins (map 9). Statewide, they hold 850 million acre-feet of water, 20 times more than the surface water supply, and enough to cover California eight feet deep. Less than half of that water is usable, however, because of poor quality and the high costs of pumping it from the ground. Surface water is found primarily in the northern half of the state, but groundwater is more evenly distributed across California. It is a valuable local source of water, because it is usually tapped close to where it is used, eliminating the need for long-distance transport facilities.

The Central Valley holds the largest groundwater basins. Much of the fresh supply there is found within alluvial deposits of sand, gravel, and silt washed down from the mountains rimming the valley. Below those freshwater-bearing deposits lies a thick layer of marine sediments, deposited when the Pacific Ocean covered that area. Deep drilling sometimes penetrates into salty groundwater trapped in the marine layer. Overdrafting of the freshwater aquifer has, in places, led to intrusion of saltwater from below as the overlying pressure dropped.

Although groundwater interacts with surface water, and

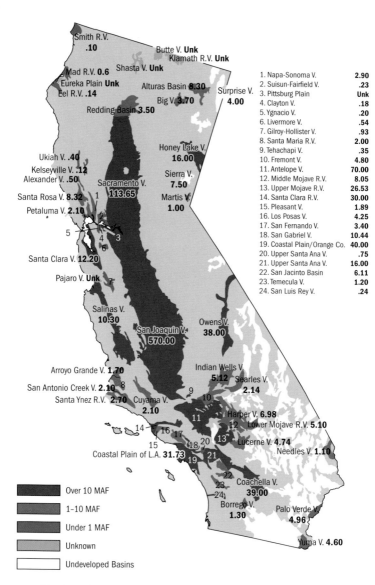

Map 9. California groundwater basins: known total storage capacity in millions of acre-feet (MAF). (Redrawn from Hundley Jr. 2001.)

Smith R.V. **.10**
Butte V. **Unk**
Klamath R.V. **Unk**
Mad R.V. **0.6**
Shasta V. **Unk**
Eureka Plain **Unk**
Eel R.V. **.14**
Alturas Basin **8.30**
Surprise V. **4.00**
Big V. **3.70**
Redding Basin **3.50**
Honey Lake V. **16.00**
Ukiah V. **.40**
Kelseyville V. **.12**
Alexander V. **.50**
Sierra V. **7.50**
Sacramento V. **113.65**
Santa Rosa **8.32**
Martis V. **1.00**
Petaluma V. **2.10**
Santa Clara V. **12.20**
Pajaro V. **Unk**
Salinas V. **10.30**
Owens V. **38.00**
San Joaquin V. **570.00**
Arroyo Grande V. **1.70**
Indian Wells V. **5.12**
San Antonio Creek V. **2.10**
Searles V. **2.14**
Santa Ynez R.V. **2.70**
Cuyama V. **2.10**
Harper V. **6.98**
Lower Mojave R.V. **5.10**
Lucerne V. **4.74**
Needles V. **1.10**
Coastal Plain of L.A. **31.73**
Coachella V. **39.00**
Borrego V. **1.30**
Palo Verde V. **4.96**
Yuma V. **4.60**

| | |
|---|---|
| 1. Napa-Sonoma V. | 2.90 |
| 2. Suisun-Fairfield V. | .23 |
| 3. Pittsburg Plain | Unk |
| 4. Clayton V. | .18 |
| 5. Ygnacio V. | .20 |
| 6. Livermore V. | .54 |
| 7. Gilroy-Hollister V. | .93 |
| 8. Santa Maria R.V. | 2.00 |
| 9. Tehachapi V. | .35 |
| 10. Fremont V. | 4.80 |
| 11. Antelope V. | 70.00 |
| 12. Middle Mojave R.V. | 8.05 |
| 13. Upper Mojave R.V. | 26.53 |
| 14. Santa Clara R.V. | 30.00 |
| 15. Pleasant V. | 1.89 |
| 16. Los Posas V. | 4.25 |
| 17. San Fernando V. | 3.40 |
| 18. San Gabriel V. | 10.44 |
| 19. Coastal Plain/Orange Co. | 40.00 |
| 20. Upper Santa Ana V. | .75 |
| 21. Upper Santa Ana V. | 16.00 |
| 22. San Jacinto Basin | 6.11 |
| 23. Temecula V. | 1.20 |
| 24. San Luis Rey V. | .24 |

Over 10 MAF
1–10 MAF
Under 1 MAF
Unknown
Undeveloped Basins

California has laws to govern every aspect of surface water use and quality, there are no statewide groundwater management laws. Land ownership, in most cases, brings with it the right to essentially unregulated pumping of groundwater.

Because it hides beneath our feet, out of sight, there are a number of common misconceptions about groundwater:

- California has no "subterranean lakes" or "underground rivers." Vast aquifer basins have been identified, but within those basins, water simply saturates pores surrounding soil particles.

- Groundwater is not locked away, separate from the rest of the water cycle. It is a renewable resource and a portion of the interconnected wheel. Though surface water and groundwater move at different speeds, with most surface water recycling far more quickly, surface and groundwater do interact. The water that seeps from an aquifer into rivers, lakes, or springs or is pumped out from wells is recharged when precipitation soaks into the ground. Around seven million acre-feet of water naturally make their way into the state's aquifers each year. Irrigation water seeps into aquifers, too, in the amount of about 6.5 million acre-feet each year. Some water agencies artificially recharge basins by flooding surface ponds or by injecting water deep into aquifers.

- Groundwater is not unlimited. Aquifers can be overdrafted when groundwater is removed faster than it can be replenished. Annual overdrafting averages about 2.2 million acre-feet across the state and about 800,000 acre-feet in the Central Valley alone.

- Percolation of groundwater through an aquifer cannot clean out any and every contaminant. Though natural filtration makes groundwater generally purer than surface water, our society has learned bitter lessons about its limitations. Specific wells or entire groundwater basins have been lost, essentially forever, to contamination.

# Hydrologic Regions

California's major drainage basins, which share similar precipitation and runoff patterns, may be grouped into 10 hydrological regions. These water-planning areas are bounded by the crests of the state's mountain ranges. Beginning in the north and working southward (as so much of the water does, these days), they are the North Coast, Sacramento River, North Lahontan, San Francisco Bay, San Joaquin River, Central Coast, Tulare Lake, South Lahontan, South Coast, and Colorado River regions (map 10). Maps of the state's geomorphic provinces and natural habitat regions look similar to those of its hydrologic regions, because topography influences climate and biological responses. The regions take in a variety of ecosystem types, however, because they include elevations that may range from above the snow line to below sea level. Each region also incorporates the watersheds of many rivers that share similar climates and generally terminate in the same place, either on the coast, at the Bay-Delta, or in inland basins.

## North Coast Region

From the Oregon border, the North Coast region extends southward through the Mendocino coast and down to Tomales Bay, north of San Francisco. It reaches inland to the crests of the Klamath Mountains and the Coast Ranges. Major cities in the region include Crescent City and Santa Rosa. Here, the highest rainfall totals in the state create California's version of rain forests, where coast redwoods (*Sequoia sempervirens*) and Douglas-firs (*Pseudotsuga menziesii*) carpet rugged mountain slopes. Much of this watershed receives over 100 inches of rain per year, and some areas near the Oregon border receive almost 200 inches.

Some winter precipitation falls as snow on the Klamath Mountains and Trinity Alps, but summer's coastal fogs are

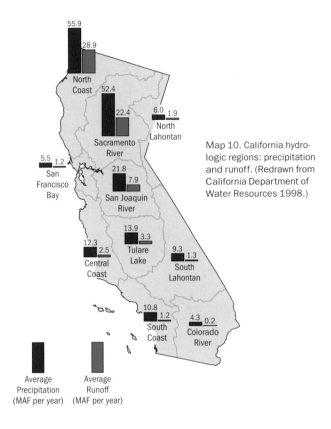

North Coast

55.9
28.9

Sacramento River

52.4
22.4

North Lahontan

6.0  1.9

San Francisco Bay

5.5  1.2

San Joaquin River

21.8
7.9

Tulare Lake

13.9
3.3

Central Coast

12.3
2.5

South Lahontan

9.3  1.3

South Coast

10.8  1.2

Colorado River

4.3  0.2

Average Precipitation (MAF per year)

Average Runoff (MAF per year)

Map 10. California hydrologic regions: precipitation and runoff. (Redrawn from California Department of Water Resources 1998.)

even more important here than the moderate snowpack of winter. Coast redwoods specialize in growing massive on long, slow drinks of harvested summer fog (pl. 27). You may feel the need for a raincoat when walking through groves of the giant trees while mists drift through their crowns. Fog collects on needles, and the forest floor is continually splattered by drips that can account for more than 30 percent of the water reaching the ground.

Plate 27. Coast redwoods slowly drinking in the summer fog.

North Coast rivers provide local water supplies; critical spawning habitat for Coho and Chinook Salmon *(Oncorhynchus kisutch* and *O. tshawytscha)*, Steelhead Trout, and other anadromous fish; commercial and sportfishing; and whitewater opportunities. They carry 40 percent of the state's runoff, averaging 28.5 million acre-feet each year. The highest flood peak discharges ever recorded in the state occurred here. North Coast rivers regularly turn brown from sediment loads during intense rain episodes, a natural condition that is exacerbated by logging and grazing practices in the watersheds.

In the far northwest corner of California, close to the Oregon border, the Smith River watershed sends the ocean the highest volumes of runoff water per acre in the state. It also has the proud, but lonely, distinction of being the only watershed of a major river in the state that is entirely free of dams.

The Klamath is California's second-largest river. With headwaters in the mountains of eastern Oregon, the Klamath irrigates farms in southern Oregon before crossing into California. It annually sends over 11 million acre-feet of water toward the Pacific Ocean, draining a 12,100-square-mile watershed that includes Redwood National Park. Portions are protected in the Wild and Scenic Rivers system. Awareness that the Klamath watershed was part of the state's waterscape increased among Californians when requirements for farmers to share water with threatened populations of anadromous fish—Steelhead, Chinook Salmon, Coho Salmon, Cutthroat Trout *(Oncorhynchus clarki)*, Green Sturgeon *(Acipenser medirostris)*, and others—turned into newsworthy standoffs between Oregon farmers and government agency personnel early in the twenty-first century.

The 170-mile-long Trinity River drains into the Klamath River, but as much as 90 percent of its water has been diverted entirely out of the North Coast drainage and into the Sacramento Valley. Salmon runs declined as a result of the reduced flows down the Trinity, affecting not only the commercial harvest, but also the subsistence and ceremonial roles the fish

Plate 28. Kayaks on the Trinity River.

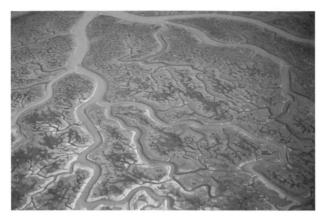

Plate 29. Humboldt Bay National Wildlife Refuge.

had for Hoopa and Yurok Indians. In-stream flow requirements have restored some of the flow down the Trinity's natural channel. Major portions of the Trinity and of its inland
tributaries, the Salmon and Scott, are part of the Wild and
Scenic Rivers system (pl. 28).

Plate 30. The Eel River.

Humboldt Bay contains the largest wetlands estuary north of San Francisco (pl. 29). From Arcata, on the bay, north of Eureka, the Mad River extends back from the sea 90 miles into the Coast Ranges. South of Eureka, the Van Duzen River passes through Humboldt Redwoods State Park and out to sea at Ferndale.

Travelers on Hwy. 101 cross and recross the winding Eel River as they travel northward through redwood forests from Weott to Fortuna. Most of the Eel is within the Wild and Scenic Rivers system (pl. 30). The peak flood discharge measured on the Eel was 753,000 cubic feet per second. This record exceeds anything that the Sacramento River has generated from its much larger watershed—an indication of the extreme rainfall events in the North Coast region.

The Mattole drains the Lost Coast between Fort Bragg and Cape Mendocino. Runoff from the mountains west of Willits comes down the Noyo through a relatively small coastal watershed, reaching Noyo Harbor at Fort Bragg. The Navarro emerges on the Mendocino coast between the towns of Mendocino and Elk, after just a 19-mile descent from its headwaters.

South of Point Arena, the Gualala River enters the sea. There was once a proposal to suck freshwater offshore from the mouths of the Gualala and the Albion, north of the Navarro, and tow it in massive bags down the coast for sale to San Diego. The idea was dropped in 2003 because of the opposition of local residents and the expense of the environmental documentation required by the California Coastal Commission and the State Water Resources Control Board (SWRCB).

Not far from Fort Ross (a historic Russian settlement established in 1812), the Russian River enters the ocean at Jenner. Its headwaters are in Mendocino County, in the hills above Ukiah. Since 1908, the Russian River has also carried some Eel River water, diverted through a tunnel from a reservoir on the headwaters of the Eel.

Plate 31. Duck club members on remnant wetlands.

## Sacramento River Region

The Sacramento River, California's largest, has a 26,548-square-mile watershed that drains the northern half of the Central Valley, with tributaries reaching toward the Oregon border and across the northeast corner of the state. The river carries 31 percent of the state's total runoff, about 22.4 million acre-feet per year. Its watershed includes the eastern slopes of the northern Coast Ranges, Mount Shasta, and the southern Cascade peaks, but it receives most of its runoff from the west slope of the Sierra Nevada. Sacramento River tributaries in the Sierra foothills became the first mining sites of the Mother Lode, where the gold rush began.

Edwin Bryant described the Sacramento River as he saw it in 1846 near Sutter's Fort, where it was "nearly half a mile in width. It is fringed with timber, chiefly oak and sycamore. Grape-vines and a variety of shrubbery ornament its banks, and give a most charming effect when sailing upon its placid and limpid current. I never saw a more beautiful stream. In the rainy season, and in the spring, when the snows on the mountains are melting, it overflows its banks in many places.

Plate 32. Sacramento Valley rice fields.

It abounds in fish, the most valuable of which is the salmon...
the largest and the fattest I have ever seen. I have seen salmon
taken from the Sacramento five feet in length. All of its tributaries are equally rich in the finny tribe" ([1848] 1985,
271–72).

The Sacramento Valley still has 175,000 acres of wetlands,
most managed by private duck clubs in the Butte, Colusa, and
American basins and the Delta (pl. 31), but this entire watershed has been transformed by 147 dams. Dams on the river
and its tributaries blocked access to most of the historic
spawning grounds for four runs of native Chinook Salmon
that once migrated by the millions to the upper watershed to
spawn. Most of the main river channel has been confined between levees. Flood control and irrigation facilities allowed
the Sacramento Valley to be transformed into one of the
world's major agricultural regions. More than 2.1 million
acres of farmland grow rice, wheat, orchard fruits, alfalfa, and
vegetable crops (pl. 32). Farmers and city residents, including
the state's legislators, live on a floodplain that used to be regularly inundated.

Plate 33. Salmon fishermen and rafters on the American River above Sacramento.

Sacramento River tributaries include several major rivers and many small creeks. The McCloud and Pit Rivers enter at Shasta Reservoir. The Pit River's 5,000-square-mile watershed spreads across much of the northeastern part of the state. Goose Lake, large but shallow, straddles the Oregon-California border; it drained toward the Pit River whenever it was full.

From Mount Lassen, Mill Creek flows down to the Sacramento River. Mill is one of the last streams in the northern Sierra that provide pristine spawning habitat for salmon and Steelhead. A few of the Sacramento's other small tributaries—Battle Creek, Antelope Creek, Deer Creek, Big Chico Creek, and Butte Creek—also remain undammed.

The Feather River is the primary water source for the State Water Project (SWP). The middle fork of the Feather, upstream from Oroville Dam, is part of the Wild and Scenic Rivers system. The Yuba and Bear River tributaries join the Feather before it reaches the Sacramento.

On the south fork of the American River, in 1848, James Marshall made a discovery that would shape much of California's early history and many environmental changes. In May of that year, entrepreneur Sam Brannan spread the news in the streets of San Francisco, shouting, "Gold! Gold! Gold from the American River!" The river had been named the Rio de los Americanos in 1837, because American trappers were frequenting that part of Mexican Alta California. It now passes through Sacramento along a 26-mile river parkway (pl. 33). The upper north fork of the American River is part of the Wild and Scenic Rivers system.

One of California's largest natural lakes, Clear Lake, is in the Coast Ranges within the Sacramento River region. With a 100-mile shoreline and 43,000 surface acres, Clear Lake is the largest freshwater lake inside California's borders (Lake Tahoe is quite a bit larger but is partly in Nevada). It is known as the Bass Capital of the West for its recreational fishing, but its age is a more venerable distinction: the lake has been there for about three million years, making it one of the oldest in North America. Water from Clear Lake reaches Cache Creek and drops into Yolo County in the Central Valley.

## North Lahontan Region

The North and South Lahontan regions are named for Lake Lahontan, the Ice Age lake that once covered 8,665 square miles of the Great Basin, with tributary streams in the Eastern Sierra. Much of the runoff from the Eastern Sierra Nevada drains into terminal lake basins in Nevada that are the isolated remnants of Lake Lahontan. The North Lahontan region extends from the Oregon border south to the Walker River watershed above Bridgeport Valley.

Lake Tahoe is Northern California's largest water feature and the dominant feature of a hydrologic region that is profoundly influenced by the Sierra rain shadow. Tahoe, between four and five million years old, is the oldest lake in North

Plate 34.
Lake Tahoe.

America. It is 22 miles long and 12 miles wide. The state line splits it from north to south, with a jog to the east in the middle of the lake that turns the boundary line to parallel the Sierra crest. The lake is 1,685 feet deep, so it never freezes, even though its surface is 6,229 feet above sea level.

An early tourist to Lake Tahoe, Mark Twain, marveled at its clarity in 1861 (pl. 34): "So singularly clear was the water, that where it was only twenty or thirty feet deep the bottom was so perfectly distinct that the boat seemed floating in the air! Yes, where it was even *eighty* feet deep. Every little pebble was distinct, every speckled trout, every hand's-breadth of sand. So empty and airy did all spaces seem below us, and so strong was the sense of floating high aloft in nothingness, that we called these boat-excursions 'balloon-voyages' " ([1872] 1972, 168–69).

Plate 35. Runoff from surrounding development entering Lake Tahoe, creating eutrophication.

As beautiful as it remains, Tahoe's clarity has been decreasing. In the 1960s, white disks used by researchers to monitor water visibility could be seen 100 feet below the surface. The disks disappear at 70 feet now, indicating that in recent decades visibility has diminished by about one foot per year. Runoff from homes, casinos, golf courses, and the streets and septic systems that service them washes nutrients into Lake Tahoe (pl. 35). Nitrogen and phosphorus fertilize algae growth in the water, which had been renowned for its near sterility. This eutrophication has been exacerbated by the loss of adjacent marshes that used to filter runoff.

Lake Tahoe's only outflow is the Truckee River. Its watershed in California drains to Winnemucca and Pyramid Lakes in Nevada. Cutthroat Trout once climbed the Truckee to spawn, coming all the way to Lake Tahoe. That population went extinct after irrigation diversions interfered with flows needed by the fish. A Cutthroat fishery was reestablished with fish brought from Walker Lake, farther south in Nevada. Another native fish (Chasmistes cujus), a sucker named Cui-ui by the local Paiute Indians, became an endangered species. In 1999, after decades of legal disputes, an allocation of water between California and Nevada provided water to protect Pyramid Lake and wildlife refuges farther downstream.

The Carson and Walker Rivers drain Eastern Sierra watersheds that also send water to wetlands and lakes in western Nevada. From headwaters near Sonora Pass and above Bridgeport, the Walker flows northward, then turns southward to terminate in Walker Lake. Diversions for agriculture after the river leaves California have caused Walker Lake to drop 140 feet since 1900. Salinity levels in the lake have increased to near the limit for freshwater fish, threatening the Cutthroat Trout and Tui Chub *(Gila bicolor)* populations. Endangered White Pelicans *(Pelecanus erythrorhynchos)* and Common Loons *(Gavia immer)* will lose an essential migration stop unless California and Nevada water rights holders begin sharing with the lake.

## San Francisco Bay Region

Cool and foggy on the coast, but with inland hills that experience the hot, dry summer weather of Mediterranean climates, the San Francisco Bay region takes in watersheds that drain into San Francisco, San Pablo, and Suisun Bays. The region's eastern boundary runs from the confluence of the Sacramento and San Joaquin Rivers along the watershed crests of the Coast Ranges, including the Berkeley and Oakland hills in the East Bay (pl. 36). In the north, the region takes in the Napa River valley and Tomales Bay. Where the San Andreas Fault enters the Pacific Ocean, Lagunitas Creek supplies the Tomales Bay estuary with freshwater gathered from Mount Tamalpais and other Marin County hillsides. Coho Salmon and Steelhead Trout in Lagunitas have declined, as have conditions for the endangered California Freshwater Shrimp *(Syncaris pacifica)*. The region extends down the San Francisco Peninsula to the Santa Cruz Mountains.

Plate 36. Egret at the Martinez Regional Shoreline, where the Carquinez Strait connects San Pablo Bay and San Francisco Bay.

Urbanization and industrial development have transformed the Bay Area wetlands and the local watersheds. Enormous growth in San Francisco, Oakland, San Jose, and their sprawling suburban satellites was only possible because of water imported from outside the local watersheds.

## San Joaquin River Region

The San Joaquin Valley is drier and hotter than the Sacramento Valley, but more than 100,000 acres of wetlands persist there, mostly managed by private duck clubs (pl. 37). The region is bounded on the west by the Diablo Range portion of the Coast Ranges and on the east by the Sierra Nevada crest. There are five million acres of irrigated farmlands in the San Joaquin Valley; Fresno and Tulare Counties are the top agricultural revenue–generating counties in the nation. Crops include cotton, corn, grains, grapes, vegetables, orchard fruits, nuts, citrus, and alfalfa (pl. 38). Water rights developed for agriculture have made the land valuable to builders, however.

Plate 37. Geese at the San Joaquin River National Wildlife Refuge near Los Banos.

Fertile farmland is rapidly succumbing to urban sprawl, repeating a pattern that completely transformed the nation's former number one agricultural region, Los Angeles County.

Groundwater is a major supply source in the San Joaquin Valley, for both agricultural and urban use. Portions of the region have experienced severe land subsidence due to groundwater overdrafting. Heavy pumping from lands between the Mokelumne and Stanislaus Rivers east of Stockton also caused poor-quality Delta water to migrate toward city wells.

The San Joaquin River watershed drains nine percent of the state's runoff water, about 6.4 million acre-feet in an average year. Its upper portion includes the west slopes of Mammoth Mountain, Devil's Postpile National Monument, and parts of the Ansel Adams Wilderness. Once the river reaches the valley, it turns sharply northward and picks up water from major tributaries as they emerge from the mountain foothills. Because about 60 miles of the San Joaquin have been dewatered since the 1940s, when Friant Dam was built and its water was diverted to farm irrigators, the only San Joaquin River

Plate 38.
Harvesting
peas in the
Central Valley.

water that normally enters the Delta is contributed by its tributaries, supplemented by farm return drainage water plus treated urban sewage.

Two of the rivers in this region, the Cosumnes and the Mokelumne, enter the Delta north of Stockton without actually joining the San Joaquin. The Cosumnes, one of the smallest Sierra Nevada rivers, is the only watershed in the western Sierra with no major dam (some small dams serve local irrigation but do not block fish passage). Without flood control structures, the river can behave naturally. In the Cosumnes Nature Preserve on the valley floor, old levees have been purposely breached, allowing the river to seasonally leave its banks and reoccupy parts of its natural floodplain. The Mokelumne River serves as the major water supply for the East Bay Municipal Utility District (EBMUD) and is also diverted near Lodi for irrigation.

The major tributaries to the San Joaquin are, from north to south, the Stanislaus, Tuolumne, and Merced Rivers. The Stanislaus drains the Sonora Pass area. Its north fork passes through Calaveras Big Trees State Park. In the 1970s, national attention became focused on New Melones Dam, whose reservoir flooded high-quality whitewater-rafting segments of the Stanislaus River canyon.

The Tuolumne River is the largest tributary to the San

Joaquin. Its headwaters are in Yosemite National Park. Snow that melts west of Tioga Pass, the eastern entrance station to the park, flows through Tuolumne Meadows, drops down dramatic cascades into the Grand Canyon of the Tuolumne, then enters Hetch Hetchy Valley. John Muir called Hetch Hetchy "the 'Tuolumne Yosemite,' for it is a wonderfully exact counterpart of the Merced Yosemite, not only in its sublime rocks and waterfalls but in the gardens, groves, and meadows of its flowery park-like floor" (1912, 187).

Today, the city of San Francisco's O'Shaughnessy Dam floods Hetch Hetchy Valley; farther downstream, New Don Pedro Reservoir diverts water to irrigation districts. There has been a severe decline in Chinook Salmon in the Tuolumne River. Fewer than 100 fall-run salmon returned to the river during 1991 and fewer than 200 in 1992, compared to a historical maximum of 130,000 in 1944.

Perhaps the most famous 2,400-foot stretch of water flowing to the Merced River is Yosemite Creek's two-stage drop over Yosemite Falls (pl. 39). Portions of the Merced may be the most visited river stretches in California, as three million tourists come to Yosemite Valley each year. Many swim and float in the Merced as it meanders through the valley, and even more hike to its waterfalls. On the main channel of the Merced, water cascades over 600-foot Nevada Falls and 317-foot Vernal Falls. Today the lower Merced River has the southernmost run of Chinook Salmon on the West Coast.

## Central Coast Region

Central Coast rivers originate in the Coast Ranges and drain to the Pacific Ocean. The region extends from Santa Cruz to Santa Barbara. Major rivers include the Carmel and the Big Sur, with headwaters in the steep mountains of the Ventana Wilderness, inland from the Big Sur coast. The Big Sur is part of the Wild and Scenic Rivers system. It was once a major spawning ground and nursery stream for Steelhead Trout,

Plate 39. Yosemite Falls.

with up to 3,000 spawners per year, but dams, diversions, and groundwater pumping along the river reduced its flows and the number of fish that successfully spawn.

The Salinas River makes a long northwesterly run to Monterey Bay. Much of the water used for agriculture in the Salinas Valley comes from groundwater replenished by the river. In *East of Eden,* John Steinbeck described the Salinas as "only a part-time river. The summer sun drove it underground. It

Plate 40. The Salinas River.

was not a fine river at all, but it was the only one we had and so we boasted about it" ([1952] 1995, 4) (pl. 40). A tributary of the Salinas, the Arroyo Seco River sustains a small population of threatened Steelhead Trout that migrate there from the ocean to spawn. Downstream of the Los Padres National Forest boundary, the Arroyo Seco floodplain waters one of the largest native sycamore forests in central California.

San Luis Obispo Creek flows out of the Santa Lucia Range, through the town of San Luis Obispo, and out to sea. Though streamflow below the town is primarily treated wastewater in the dry season, the drainage still supports populations of Southwestern Pond Turtles *(Clemmys marmorata pallida),* Red-legged Frogs *(Rana aurora dratonii),* and one of the southerly races of Steelhead.

The Santa Ynez River drains the rugged mountains of the same name north of Santa Barbara. The upper Santa Ynez River has Southern California's longest stretch of free-flowing river accessible to recreational users. Historically, the Santa Ynez supported the largest run of Steelhead Trout in Southern California, but the too-common story of reduced flows, high temperatures, and barriers to migration also occurred in this drainage.

# Tulare Lake Region

The southern third of the Central Valley contains the Tulare Lake basin. The Tehachapi Mountains form the region's southern boundary. Here the valley floor receives less than 10 inches of rain; Bakersfield averages only six inches of winter rain. Tulare Basin rivers never reached the sea. The Kern River once terminated in Buena Vista Lake, and the Tule, Kings, and Kaweah Rivers (from the Sequoia National Park area) once formed Tulare Lake. All of those rivers have stretches below the foothills that are now completely dewatered.

James Carson, in 1852, wrote about

> the placid blue water of the Tulare Lake, whose ripples wash the foot of the low hills of the Coast range…. [Tulare Lake] is about fifty miles in length by thirty in width…. Buena Vista Lake is a beautiful sheet of water, twenty miles long, and from five to ten in width; it lays nestled in the head of the valley…. The slough connecting the Tulare and Buena Vista Lakes is about eighty miles in length…. Thousands of wild horses subsist on the grasses growing there now…. Every beast and bird of the chase and hunt is to be found in abundance on the Tulares. Horses, cattle, elk, antelope, black tail and red deer, grizzly and brown bear, black and grey wolves, coyotes, ocelots, California lions, wildcats, beaver, otter, mink, weasels, ferrets, hare, rabbits, grey and red foxes, grey and ground squirrels, kangaroo rats, badgers, skunks, muskrats, hedgehogs, and many species of small animals…; swan, geese, brant, and over twenty different…ducks…in countless myriads from the first of October until the first of April, besides millions of…crane, plover, snipe, and quail. (65–66, 68–69, 76, 80)

Carson was describing the largest single block of wetland habitat in California, approximately 500,000 acres. Currently there are only about 6,400 acres of flooded wetland habitat left in the basin, mostly in the Kern and Pixley National Wildlife Refuges. Tulare and Buena Vista Lakes have vanished

*Above:*
Plate 41. Cotton harvest in the Tulare Basin.

*Right:*
Plate 42. Bubbs Creek, a tributary of the Kings River, in Kings Canyon National Park.

from maps of the southern Central Valley, their river tributaries diverted and the lakebeds transformed into farm fields (pl. 41). Still, in about one-third of winters the basin experiences flooding. Lakebed farmers must also contend with salt buildup in the soil. That is something that all irrigators must address, but it is exacerbated in the Tulare Basin, because the topsoil sits above an impermeable layer that does not allow drainage. Salts increase unless they are flushed away with lots of water. The wastewater settles into sinks, where toxic chemicals can become a hazard for wildlife.

Upper portions of the Kings River are in Kings Canyon National Park and were added to the Wild and Scenic Rivers system in 1987 (pl. 42). The Kings carves away at one of the deepest canyons in North America as it drops more than 13,000 feet. In the valley, it is diverted into a system of irrigation channels and only deposits water on the Tulare Lake bed in extremely wet years.

The Tule River, a tributary of the Kings, has headwaters in the Golden Trout Wilderness of the southern Sierra. One fork passes through the recently designated Sequoia National Monument, east of Porterville.

Snowmelt from Mount Whitney, in Sequoia National Park, forms part of the water entering the Kern River. The upper portions of the Kern are part of the Wild and Scenic Rivers system. The south fork and Golden Trout Creek have populations of Golden Trout *(Salmo aguabonita)*, the only native trout found in the southern Sierra (pl. 43). California's largest lowland riparian forest is found along the south fork, upstream from Lake Isabella. The American Bird Conservancy has identified Kern River Preserve, also on the south fork, as a Globally Important Bird Area; it attracts over 300 species of birds, including Yellow-billed Cuckoo *(Coccyzus americanus occidentalis)* and Willow Flycatcher *(Empidonax traillii)*. Stretches of the Kern River below Isabella Dam are popular for whitewater rafting (but flows vary according to releases from the reservoir). Downstream diversions cause

Plate 43. Golden Trout, the California state fish.

the Kern to go dry, but efforts are being made to put water back into the river as it passes through Bakersfield, using groundwater from local wells.

## South Lahontan Region

At the Sierra crest, snow and ice loom over a sudden plummet into eastern high desert basins. This region contains the highest and lowest points in the lower 48 states: Mount Whitney, at 14,495 feet above sea level, and not far away, Death Valley, 282 feet below sea level. Owens Valley is a 90-mile-long trough nestled between the Sierra Nevada and the White and Inyo mountain ranges. The Owens River carries snow water the length of the valley to Owens Lake. Farther north, in a separate drainage basin, five smaller streams terminate at Mono Lake, where, according to John Muir, "spirit-like, our happy stream vanishes in vapor, and floats free again in the sky" (1961, 71). The Mojave Desert dominates the southern parts of the region. Using water imported from the Sacramento Valley, cities like Lancaster and Palmdale, in Los Angeles County, and Victorville and Apple Valley, in San Bernardino County, have grown tremendously in the past few decades. The populations of Inyo and Mono Counties, in the Eastern

Plate 44. Tufa towers at Mono Lake.

Sierra, are essentially stable because aqueduct facilities export water from that region to Los Angeles.

Mono Lake is a vast inland sea that supports migratory and nesting bird populations attracted by the lake's enormous productivity. Harsh alkaline water, almost three times as salty as the ocean, provides nutrients to algae, brine shrimp, and Alkali Flies (*Ephydra hians*). The ancient lake, at least one million years old, has been declared an Outstanding Natural Resource Water by the Environmental Protection Agency and a Globally Important Bird Area by the American Bird Conservancy. Its unique chemical "recipe" has produced a unique ecosystem, a good example of the critical role water plays in shaping plant and animal responses. It is a "three-salt lake," containing carbonates, chlorides, and sulfates. To mimic the mixture requires table salt, baking soda, and Epsom salts in the right proportions. Because carbonates predominate, photogenic limestone tufa towers form where freshwater springs (bearing calcium) enter the carbonate-rich lake (pl. 44).

Mono Lake became the center of a major controversy after decades of stream diversions to Los Angeles caused it to shrink. To stop the decline before the lake became lethally concentrated, a court directed the State Water Resources Control Board to amend Los Angeles's water licenses. Since 1941, four of the lake's tributary streams, Lee Vining, Rush, Walker, and Parker Creeks, had been completely dewatered by diversions into the Los Angeles Aqueduct system. That violation of state fish and game law was also corrected by the 1994 SWRCB plan implementing the court order.

In 1913, three decades before the Los Angeles Aqueduct system tapped into Mono Basin streams, water from the Owens River had begun flowing to Los Angeles. Owens Lake dried up within a decade, and the agricultural valley was transformed into a "wholly owned subsidiary" of the city of Los Angeles (pls. 45, 46). Dust storms blowing off the desiccated lakebed began violating state air quality standards, forcing the city to put a portion of the Owens River water back into the lakebed as the twenty-first century opened.

Water in the north fork of the Owens River, at 9,500 feet above sea level, was the best John Muir ever found, he wrote in 1901. "It is not only delightfully cool and bright, but brisk, sparkling, exhilarating, and so positively delicious to the taste that a party of friends I led to it twenty five years ago still praise it, and refer to it as 'that wonderful champagne water;' though, comparatively, the finest wine is a coarse and vulgar drink" (185).

Although trout fishing is today a major recreation activity in Eastern Sierra streams and lakes, there were no native trout in any of these waters; all have been introduced. The only fish in the Owens River system were the Owens Sucker *(Catostomus fumeiventris),* which used the river as far up as Convict Lake; the small Speckled Dace *(Rhinichthys osculus);* and the Owens Pupfish *(Cyprinodon radiosus).*

The dace and pupfish are also found in the Amargosa River, which flows southward from Nevada into California, then turns westward into the Mojave Desert and, finally, northward into Death Valley. It flows intermittently, but a 20-mile seg-

Plate 45. Owens Lake before the Los Angeles Aqueduct began diversions.

Plate 46. The bed of Owens Lake today.

ment near the town of Shoshone is perennial. "Amargosa" is Spanish for "bitter water," but the water has critical importance to desert wildlife and plants. Its riparian habitat supports endangered and threatened birds, including the Willow Flycatcher, Yellow-billed Cuckoo, and Least Bell's Vireo *(Vireo bellii pusillus)* (pl. 47). The Amargosa Vole *(Microtus californicus scirpensis)* is found nowhere else in the world.

Plate 47. Western Yellow-billed Cuckoo, shown here in riparian habitat at the Kern River Preserve.

The Mojave River drops out of the San Bernardino Mountains and flows eastward, going underground as it enters the desert. The river and the Mojave groundwater basin act as one interacting water source.

## South Coast Region

Rivers and creeks in the Southern California coastal basins drain into the Pacific Ocean. This is the West Coast's most populated, most urbanized region. While more than 50 percent of California's population lives here, the area naturally receives less than two percent of the state's precipitation. It would be unable to support even a significant fraction of its population without water imported from other regions of California and the Colorado River. The hydrologic region is bounded in the north by the Santa Barbara–Ventura County line and the San Gabriel and San Bernardino Mountains. The eastern boundary is formed by the San Jacinto and Santa Rosa

Plate 48.
Artesian well
near San
Bernardino,
about 1900.

Mountains, then the Peninsular Ranges down to the Mexican
border.

Rainfall across Southern California is quite variable. Seasonal averages depend on elevation and topography. Los Angeles gets 15 inches of rain downtown but only eight inches
along the coast. At the summit of the San Gabriel Mountains,
40 inches may fall. Groundwater basins were once so full that
they produced artesian wells, particularly around San Bernardino and in northwestern Orange County (pl. 48). The
basins became badly overdrawn early in the twentieth century.

So much of the watershed has been covered by concrete,
asphalt, and buildings that stormwater does not percolate
into the ground but rapidly runs into channels and drains.
That not only reduces groundwater recharge but carries trash
and toxic chemicals to the ocean and beaches.

Much of the Southern California population seems unaware of the remnants of the former riparian corridors, and
equally unaware that those local channels once supported
populations of Steelhead and Pacific Lamprey, suckers, native
frogs, and Southwestern Pond Turtles. The rivers of the
Southland are typically small, ephemeral, and intermittent,

Plate 49. The channelized Santa Ana River.

but, ironically, many of them carry *more* water today than they did before imported water arrived in great quantities in Southern California. Wastewater from millions of people must go somewhere after it passes through treatment plants. "Effluent-dominant" rivers that would naturally be dry except during the rainy season now run all year with treated wastewater.

The 51-mile-long Los Angeles River now flows mostly through 470 miles of concrete channels and drains, once it drops from headwaters in the San Gabriel Mountains, Santa Susanna Mountains, Simi Hills, and Santa Monica Mountains. A major groundwater basin in the San Fernando Valley also feeds the river. It enters the ocean at the Los Angeles–Long Beach harbor, through a three-mile-long estuary.

William Mulholland, the city water engineer who oversaw the creation of the Los Angeles Aqueduct, began his career tending water ditches along the river. "The Los Angeles River was the greatest attraction," he told an oral historian in 1931. "It was a beautiful, limpid little stream with willows on its banks" (Spriggs 1931, 67). Winter rains, however, produced regular flooding, when the river would romp across the floodplain. Now and then, it completely changed its outlet, draining to the ocean through Ballona Creek.

To the south, the San Gabriel River enters the ocean at Seal Beach and Los Alamitos Bay, north of the Santa Ana River. The Santa Ana's headwaters in the San Bernardino Mountains are still free flowing, but it is channelized for most of its length through Orange County (pl. 49).

From southwestern Riverside County, the Santa Margarita River heads south for San Diego County, then bends westward and passes through the U.S. Marine Corps base at Camp Pendleton to the Pacific Ocean. One of the last free-flowing rivers in Southern California, the 27-mile-long Santa Margarita is a remnant treasure in this region that has been so urbanized and transformed.

There are amazing waterfalls in eastern San Diego County on the upper San Diego River and its tributary, Cedar Creek. The San Diego Mission sits high on a hill overlooking the historic channel of the San Diego River, but the city now occupies much of the floodplain.

## Colorado River Region

In the dry southeast corner of the state, an insignificant amount of drainage from California enters the Colorado River, which gets the overwhelming portion of its water from watersheds far to the north in the Rocky Mountains. The Colorado River is 1,440 miles long. Its watershed covers one-twelfth the area of the lower 48 states, passing through parts of Wyoming, Colorado, Utah, New Mexico, Nevada, and Arizona (pl. 50). It forms the border between California and Arizona and finally heads toward the Gulf of California in northern Mexico. The mighty Colorado only reaches the gulf in very wet years, because of the cumulative diversions north and south of the border.

Naturally high sediment loads give the river a reddish color, which is responsible for its Spanish name. Before Colorado River water is used for domestic purposes, it is often blended with purer sources to reduce salt concentrations.

The region's other dominant water body is the Salton Sea, which looms large on California maps. Even bigger than Lake

Plate 50. The Colorado River at Picacho State Park.

Tahoe, the Salton Sea stretches across 35 miles of desert and covers 360 square miles. It is 228 feet below sea level. An accidental re-creation of natural flood events that occurred many times, the sea has become a key alternative for the lost waterfowl habitat along the Southern California coast and in the Colorado River delta. Millions of birds of over 400 species visit it each year. Farm runoff keeps it full but also aggravates salinity issues. The sea suffers from a constant salt influx from the Colorado River plus added salts and fertilizers from farm runoff. It is approaching salt levels at which its prolific fish populations may no longer survive. Salinity issues will be aggravated if plans to fallow farmland and divert water to

Southern California cities are carried out. Though the farm drainage water increases the salinity of the sea, the fallowing plan would accelerate the process by diverting water to the cities. Without the water to replace evaporation, the salt lake would rapidly become more concentrated.

Today only about 36 percent of the state's surface water still keeps river and riparian ecosystems functioning. Most water moves across California in man-made channels that have facilitated population growth and development. The plumbing has become so thorough that today, almost all Californians are closely connected to one another through their water pipes.

*The water I will draw tomorrow from my tap in Malibu is today crossing the Mojave Desert from the Colorado River, and I like to think about exactly where that water is. The water I will drink tonight in a restaurant in Hollywood is by now well down the Los Angeles Aqueduct from the Owens River, and I also think about exactly where that water is: I particularly like to imagine it as it cascades down the 45-degree stone steps that aerate Owens water after its airless passage through the mountain pipes and siphons.*

—JOAN DIDION, *THE WHITE ALBUM*

# Expanding Watersheds

Stand at the top of a snow-covered ski run on the summit of Mammoth Mountain in the winter, and think about where the water under your feet may be by midsummer. Much of what drains eastward will end up in Los Angeles instead of Owens Lake. Turn around for a view of the western slope; there water will run down to the San Joaquin River. Some of the river water may reach the Central Valley and turn northward toward San Francisco Bay. Most of it, however, will be diverted onto farm fields in the San Joaquin Valley.

Plate 51. Spring snow conditions near Tioga Pass, west of the Yosemite National Park entrance.

Or get out of your car at Tioga Pass, at the eastern entrance to Yosemite National Park. Melting snow that drains westward from here will feed the Tuolumne River, which merges with San Joaquin River water flowing toward the sea (pl. 51). But much of the Tuolumne water will go, instead, into San Francisco's water supply system. Walk just a few steps outside the park and the drainage begins sloping to the east. Snowmelt from here may reach Lee Vining Creek, a tributary to Mono Lake, but some will be diverted and become the northernmost water entering the Los Angeles Aqueduct.

Drive Interstate 80 from Reno, Nevada, toward San Francisco. The American and Yuba Rivers flow westward, paralleling this route through the mountains, also aiming for the Pacific Ocean via the Golden Gate. Much of that water will be diverted out of the Delta and moved southward to irrigate crops in the San Joaquin Valley.

Farther north, the Feather River is the source for the State Water Project's California Aqueduct. Much of that water will emerge from Southern California faucets after traveling over 600 miles through natural channels and aqueducts. Some water brought to Southern California cities covers even greater distances, starting 1,400 miles away in the Colorado River headwaters in Colorado and Wyoming. Winter snowfall in the Sierra Nevada is more critical than local rainfall to the Bay Area's water supply, and both Sierra Nevada and Rocky Mountain winters are far more critical than local weather to Southern Californians.

Because of long-distance aqueducts, the great majority of Californians live within "virtual watersheds," with distant snowpacks and long-distance transportation systems providing most of their water. (Map 11.) Sierra Nevada and Rocky Mountain snow assures the economic wealth of California, a state with the world's fifth-largest economy, bigger than almost every *nation*'s. The enormous population growth of Southern California and the San Francisco Bay Area was only made possible by damming distant rivers and importing their water, so that local resource limits could be made irrelevant. Without outside water, there could only be about three million people in Southern California, where 18 million now reside from Ventura down to San Diego.

Because California's water landscape has been reengineered, about 75 percent of the *demand* for water originates south of Sacramento, although 75 percent of the water *supply*

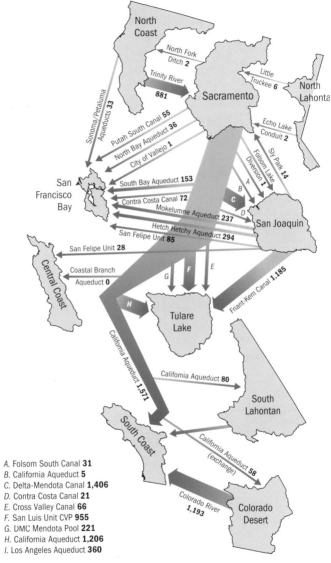

North Coast

North Fork Ditch **2**

Trinity River **881**

Sacramento

Little Truckee **6**

North Lahontan

Sonoma/Petaluma Aqueducts **33**

Putah South Canal **55**

North Bay Aqueduct **36**

City of Vallejo **1**

Echo Lake Conduit **2**

Folsom Lake Diversion **1**

Sly Park **14**

San Francisco Bay

South Bay Aqueduct **153**

Contra Costa Canal **72**

Mokelumne Aqueduct **237**

A

B

C

D

Hetch Hetchy Aqueduct **294**

San Felipe Unit **85**

San Joaquin

San Felipe Unit **28**

Central Coast

Coastal Branch Aqueduct **0**

G

F

E

Friant-Kern Canal **1,185**

H

Tulare Lake

California Aqueduct **1,571**

California Aqueduct **80**

South Lahontan

California Aqueduct (exchange) **58**

South Coast

Colorado River **1,193**

Colorado Desert

A. Folsom South Canal **31**
B. California Aqueduct **5**
C. Delta-Mendota Canal **1,406**
D. Contra Costa Canal **21**
E. Cross Valley Canal **66**
F. San Luis Unit CVP **955**
G. DMC Mendota Pool **221**
H. California Aqueduct **1,206**
I. Los Angeles Aqueduct **360**

Map 11. Regional water imports and exports, at 1995 level of development (thousands of acre-feet per year). (Redrawn from California Department of Water Resources 1998.)

in the state comes from north of the capital city. To create twenty-first-century California, an intricate network has been engineered across the face of the state (map 12). Of the 42 million acre-feet of "developed water"—water that has been gathered behind dams, pumped from the ground, and transmitted along aqueducts and through pipes—about 80 percent irrigates the state's farms, and the rest "irrigates" the urban population and its industrial needs (fig. 6).

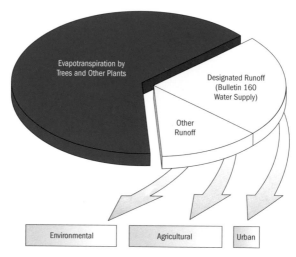

Fig. 6. Disposition of California's average annual precipitation. (Redrawn from California Department of Water Resources 1998.)

Six major systems of aqueducts and associated infrastructure redistribute water within California: the State Water Project, the Central Valley Project, a number of Colorado River delivery systems, the Los Angeles Aqueduct, the Tuolumne River/Hetch Hetchy system, and the Mokelumne Aqueduct to the East Bay. The state, federal, and regional agencies that operate these transportation systems are, in most cases, wholesalers that pass their life-giving product on to hundreds of local districts for delivery to retail consumers.

Map 12. Major water transport systems.
(Redrawn from California Department of Water
Resources 1998 and from McClurg 2000b.)

# The State Water Project

The DWR operates the massive California State Water Project (SWP), the largest state-built multipurpose water project in the United States (maps 13, 14). The SWP moves water from the Feather River watershed in the Sacramento Valley to urban and industrial consumers (70 percent of its contracts) and the balance to agricultural irrigation districts (mostly in Kern County in the San Joaquin Valley). More than two-thirds of Californians receive some of their water from the SWP. About 2.3 million acre-feet are delivered in average years, although the overcommitted system has contracted to deliver 4.2 million acre-feet.

Twenty-nine agencies hold those contracts for SWP water. The contractors cover the SWP's major operating costs and have slowly chipped away at the $1.75 billion bond debt that funded the initial construction. Since 1960, the SWP has built 29 dams, 18 pumping plants, five hydroelectric power plants, and about 600 miles of canals and pipelines. Four additional combination pumping/generating plants move water uphill into storage basins when electricity costs are low (off-peak hours), then generate power by releasing the same water through turbines during peak energy demand periods.

The SWP system begins 600 miles north of its southernmost service area with the Lake Davis, Frenchman Lake, and Antelope Lake reservoirs on upper tributaries of the Feather River (pls. 52, 53). Oroville Dam, where the Feather River passes out of the foothills, forms the largest SWP reservoir (pl. 54). The dam towers 770 feet above the riverbed; it is the tallest in the United States. When full, its reservoir covers 15,000 acres with 165 miles of shoreline, and holds 3.5 million acre-feet (2.7 million acre-feet for water supply, 800,000 acre-feet for flood control). A power plant is located *underneath* the reservoir to maximize hydroelectric generation. It is an eerie feeling to visit that plant and know you are standing beneath hundreds of feet of water.

A. = Aqueduct
P. = Power Plant
P.G.P. = Pumping Generating Plant
P.P. = Pumping Plant

Sacramento R.
Thermalito Diversion Dam P.
Thermalito P.G.P.
Thermalito Afterbay
Barker Slough P.P.
Cordelia P.P.
North Bay A.
Banks P.P.
South Bay A.
Lake Del Valle
San Luis Res.
Dos Amigos P.P.
Hyatt P.
Lake Oroville
Antelope Lake
Lake Davis
Frenchman Lake
Feather R.
Clifton Court Forebay
South Bay P.P.
Bethany Res.
Del Valle P.P.
Gianelli P.G.P.
O'Neill Forebay
California A.
Las Perillas P.P.
Badger Hill P.P.
Devil's Den P.P.
Bluestone P.P.
Polonio Pass P.P.
Coastal Branch A.
Buena Vista P.P.
Teerink P.P.
Chrisman P.P.
Edmonston P.P.
Alamo P.
Pearblossom P.P.
Mojave Siphon P.
Castaic Lake
Silverwood Lake
Devil Canyon P.
East Branch A.
Lake Perris
Oso P.P.
Quail Lake
Warne P.
Pyramid Lake
Castaic P.
West Branch A.

Map 13. State Water Project facilities.
(Redrawn from two maps in California
Department of Water Resources 1998.)

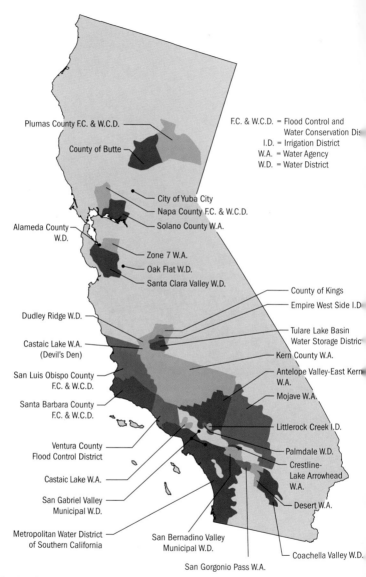

Plumas County F.C. & W.C.D.

County of Butte

City of Yuba City
Napa County F.C. & W.C.D.
Solano County W.A.

Alameda County
W.D.

Zone 7 W.A.
Oak Flat W.D.
Santa Clara Valley W.D.

Dudley Ridge W.D.

Castaic Lake W.A.
(Devil's Den)

San Luis Obispo County
F.C. & W.C.D.

Santa Barbara County
F.C. & W.C.D.

Ventura County
Flood Control District

Castaic Lake W.A.

San Gabriel Valley
Municipal W.D.

Metropolitan Water District
of Southern California

San Bernadino Valley
Municipal W.D.

San Gorgonio Pass W.A.

F.C. & W.C.D. = Flood Control and
Water Conservation Dis
I.D. = Irrigation District
W.A. = Water Agency
W.D. = Water District

County of Kings
Empire West Side I.D
Tulare Lake Basin
Water Storage Distric
Kern County W.A.
Antelope Valley-East Kern
W.A.
Mojave W.A.

Littlerock Creek I.D.

Palmdale W.D.
Crestline-
Lake Arrowhead
W.A.
Desert W.A.

Coachella Valley W.D.

Map 14. State Water Project
service areas. (Redrawn from
Hundley Jr. 2001.)

*Above:* Plate 52. Lake Davis, in the headwaters region of the Feather River and the SWP.

*Left:* Plate 53. Antelope Dam and Lake, in the headwaters region of the Feather River and the SWP.

Plate 54. Oroville, the primary SWP storage reservoir for Feather River water.

SWP water travels from the Lake Oroville reservoir along the natural channel of the Feather River and enters the Sacramento River. At the Sacramento–San Joaquin Delta some is pumped into the North Bay Aqueduct toward Napa and Solano Counties. More is diverted by powerful pumps at the Harvey O. Banks Delta Pumping Plant, which pull the SWP's allotment of Delta water into the Bethany Reservoir and the start of the California Aqueduct. In an average year, about 2.1 million acre-feet (of the 2.3 million total) are extracted here from the Delta. The 444-mile-long "Governor Edmund G. Brown California Aqueduct," to use its formal name, extends southward along the west side of the San Joaquin Valley as a concrete-lined, open canal (pl. 55). Bethany Reservoir is also the point where water is pumped into a side branch, the South Bay Aqueduct, which heads for Alameda and Santa Clara Counties.

Plate 55. The California Aqueduct south of the Delta.

Plate 56. The San Luis Reservoir, which stores both SWP and CVP water.

Sixty-three miles to the south is San Luis Reservoir, off Hwy. 152 below Pacheco Pass in the Diablo Range (pl. 56). Water is pumped uphill into this off-stream storage facility. The reservoir, its forebay, and its pumping plants are jointly operated by DWR and the federal Central Valley Project (CVP). (CVP water moves from the Delta to this location in a separate, parallel aqueduct, the Delta-Mendota Canal.) Southward, for 103 miles, the aqueduct carries both "kinds" of water.

The California Aqueduct parallels Interstate 5, passing beneath that other important transportation corridor several times (pl. 57). The Coastal Branch Aqueduct splits away, 185 miles south of the Delta, to direct some water toward the coastal cities of San Luis Obispo, Santa Maria, and Santa Bar-

Plate 57. Dos Amigos Pumping Plant on the California Aqueduct, which parallels Interstate 5 in the Central Valley.

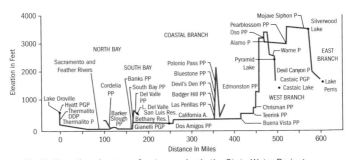

Fig. 7. Elevation changes of water moving in the State Water Project.

Plate 58. The A.D. Edmonston Pumping Plant, which lifts SWP water almost 2,000 feet over the Tehachapi Mountains.

bara. Central Coast voters decided to fund this artery during the drought that ended in 1993.

The balance of SWP water flows to the south end of the San Joaquin Valley, where it encounters a 2,000-foot-tall barrier, the Tehachapi Mountains (fig. 7). Here the A. D. Edmonston Pumping Plant lifts the water 1,926 feet into 10 miles of tunnels and siphons that pass through the mountains (pl. 58). The SWP is California's largest energy consumer, and this pumping plant burns more energy than any other single user or facility in the state. Although the hydroelectric generating plants of the SWP can, together, generate 5.8 billion kilowatt-hours per year (2.2 billion kilowatt-hours at the Oroville reservoir alone), that is only three-fourths of the electricity consumed in lifting SWP water uphill through the Central Valley and making the massive lift over the Tehachapis. Water

Plate 59. Pyramid Dam and Reservoir, with Interstate 5 in the background.

Plate 60. Castaic Pumping Plant on the west branch of the California Aqueduct, after it enters Southern California.

Plate 61. People playing in Castaic Lake, the terminal reservoir on the west branch of the California Aqueduct.

Plate 62. California Aqueduct and new housing made possible by its water deliveries to the Mojave Desert.

is heavy! Carry an eight-pound gallon bucket or jug the next time you go upstairs to better appreciate that fact. Each acre-foot demands 3,000 kilowatt-hours of electricity to overcome the Tehachapis and be redistributed to the Southland.

Below the Tehachapis, the California Aqueduct divides. The west branch stores water in the Castaic and Pyramid Lake reservoirs in north Los Angeles County to serve coastal cities (pls. 59–61). The east branch flows by the Mojave Desert city of Palmdale, in the Antelope Valley, and stores water in the Silverwood Lake reservoir in the San Bernardino Mountains (pls. 62, 63). The final SWP facility in this long chain of trans-

Plate 63. Silverwood Lake, an SWP reservoir in the San Bernardino Mountains.

Plate 64. Windsurfer on Lake Perris, the terminal reservoir on the east branch of the California Aqueduct.

portation infrastructure is Lake Perris, a reservoir in Riverside County (pl. 64). The Metropolitan Water District of Southern California (MWD) is the largest SWP contractor, taking more than two million acre-feet each year (48 percent of the SWP's contracted water).

The DWR operates three SWP visitor centers for the public: Lake Oroville Visitors Center, Romero Visitors Center at San Luis Reservoir, and Vista del Lago at Pyramid Lake.

One of the surreal circumstances shaping California water policy is that the SWP cannot actually deliver the amounts in its contracts. This has created "paper water," as opposed to the essence of real life, "wet" water. Paper water must not be used as the supply basis for authorizing new developments, nor marketed in water transfers. Paper water, if viewed as a legal entitlement, would drive bad government planning and policies by forcing the real world to accommodate to hydrological wishful thinking. (Table 2.)

# The Central Valley Project

The CVP was conceived to tame seasonal flooding and to shift water southward to irrigate three million acres of drier farmlands (15 percent of the CVP goes to urban/industrial uses). President Franklin D. Roosevelt signed the measure that authorized the CVP and transformed the Central Valley into one of the most important agricultural regions on Earth. The CVP is operated by the U.S. Bureau of Reclamation (although some of the facilities were built by the Army Corps of Engineers). One of the largest water systems in the world, it stores seven million acre-feet, or about 17 percent of the state's developed water, and delivers it to 139 landowners and eight water districts (map 15).

Broader in scope and scale than the SWP (which primarily draws on the Feather River watershed), the CVP dams and diverts water from five major rivers: the Trinity (Trinity Dam), the Sacramento (Shasta Dam), the American (Folsom Dam), the Stanislaus (New Melones Dam), and the San Joaquin (Friant Dam). One of its original goals was to end groundwater overdrafting in the southern half of the Central Valley. Instead, more acreage went into production after CVP water became available, and groundwater pumping actually increased.

Friant Dam, on the San Joaquin River, was completed in 1944, forming Millerton Lake. This was the first of 20 reservoirs in the CVP, which also includes 11 power plants and three fish hatcheries. Shasta Dam spanned the Sacramento River in 1945 (pl. 65). The canal system to deliver irrigation water from Shasta to the San Joaquin Valley opened in 1951. The CVP also dammed the Trinity River and, in 1963, began shipping that water out of the North Coast region to Whiskeytown Reservoir, which passes it along to Shasta.

Keswick Dam, nine miles below Shasta, evens out the flow from variable releases through the upstream power plants. Fish-trapping facilities there catch salmon and move them into the nearby Coleman Fish Hatchery, operated by the U.S. Fish and Wildlife Service.

Red Bluff Diversion Dam raises the Sacramento River 17 feet, creating a gravity "head" so water will leave the river and enter the Tehama-Colusa and Corning Canals. One-third of the river's water is diverted into those canals to irrigate 300,000 acres of farmland and provide seasonal water to several national wildlife refuges along the west side of the Sacramento Valley. Red Bluff Dam's fish ladders were never effective, and the dam became a major barrier to migrating fish. After years of court fighting, the dam's gates are now kept open eight months of the year, and the intake to the canals has been reengineered with improved fish screens.

Water stored behind Shasta Dam can be moved 450 miles to Bakersfield, traveling the first leg of that journey in the Sacramento River itself. At Sacramento, American River water stored behind Folsom Dam is added. About 2.5 million acre-feet are pumped annually from the Delta at the Tracy

Map 15. Central Valley Project
facilities. (Redrawn from
Hundley Jr. 2001.)

Plate 65. Shasta Dam and Reservoir with Mt. Shasta in the distance.

Plate 66. Pumping from the Delta into the Delta-Mendota Canal, part of the CVP.

Pumping Plant (not far from the SWP pumps that serve the California Aqueduct) into the Delta-Mendota Canal. Some CVP water is stored in San Luis Reservoir and, from there, shares space within the California Aqueduct, which parallels the Delta-Mendota Canal (pl. 66) but heads farther south.

New Melones Dam on the Stanislaus River was completed in 1979. Before the gates were closed to impound the Stanislaus, a fight developed, because the reservoir would flood a spectacular river canyon that, among other values, was popular for white-water rafting. New Melones Reservoir was filled in 1982.

Just below the confluence of the north and middle forks of the American River, construction of the Auburn Dam began in 1974, but it was halted the next year because of seismic risks. Plans for that dam, in a number of manifestations, remain a "never-ending story" in California's perennial water debates.

Operation of the CVP has generated controversies about environmental degradation, the prices charged (or subsidies given) to farmers, and lax enforcement of acreage limitations. Bureau of Reclamation water was meant to serve farms limited to 160 acres, to encourage small farmers who lived on their land. That type of land ownership was never the broad pattern in California, however. Under Spanish and Mexican land grants, just a few individuals owned large ranches. Federal land grants later transferred 11 percent of California's acreage to railroads; much of that land spanned the Central Valley. A few entrepreneurs manipulated federal homestead, timber, and swampland programs to circumvent acreage limits and acquire massive parcels. Henry Miller and Charles Lux ultimately controlled about 750,000 acres along both sides of the San Joaquin River for 100 miles, plus a 50-mile stretch along the Kern River. Similarly, James Ben Ali Haggin acquired more than 400,000 acres in the Central Valley. A transition from a few large landholdings to many smaller farms was conceivable, but the vision of many thousands of farms limited to 160 acres was never actually realized.

In 1982, a reform act increased CVP acreage limitations to 960 acres and dropped the former residency requirement. Today, however, 80 percent of the huge farms still exceed 1,000 acres.

Another major reform came in 1992, when the Central Valley Project Improvement Act (CVPIA) elevated fish and wildlife protection and restoration to primary purposes of the

CVP. To correct environmental damage, including endangered species designations for native fish, 800,000 acre-feet of annual runoff were dedicated back to the environment (600,000 acre-feet in dry years). Also, CVP contractors were allowed to market water to buyers outside the CVP service area.

One of the biggest environmental consequences of the CVP was not corrected by the CVPIA. At Friant Dam the entire flow of the San Joaquin River is diverted into the Friant-Kern and Madera Canals. The Friant-Kern Canal travels southward 152 miles from Friant Dam, and the Madera Canal extends 36 miles northward. A little water is allowed down the San Joaquin River channel for 28 miles, to Gravelly Ford, to serve users holding priority riparian rights, but from there the channel goes dry until Mendota Pool. (Pl. 67.)

Mendota Pool is a strange place in California's redesigned waterscape. There the Delta-Mendota Canal delivers Sacramento River water to serve CVP "exchange contractors." Irrigators in the San Joaquin Valley who held water rights to the San Joaquin River's natural flow agreed to accept this alternate CVP water, provided as the highest-priority right coming out of the Delta. They take delivery of their exchange water at Mendota Pool (pl. 68) and soon divert it to farm fields. The San Joaquin channel dries up again not far below Mendota. Other than in very wet years, the San Joaquin River is actually *not* a river for about 60 miles, until the Merced enters its channel with a transfusion from the Yosemite watershed. The Tuolumne and Stanislaus add their water farther north. Some agricultural drainage water is returned to the channel, carrying salts, fertilizers, and pesticides, and some treated municipal effluent is returned as well. The San Joaquin River, before it finds its rather pitiful way to the Delta, has been called "the lower colon of California."

Of course, after the CVP diverted the San Joaquin's water to grow crops, other life that depended on the river diminished or disappeared. In particular, 100,000 salmon could no

Plate 67. The Friant-Kern Canal, heading southward below Friant Dam and leaving very little water for the San Joaquin River, seen in the distance.

Plate 68. Mendota Pool, where Sacramento River water taken from the Delta is delivered to the dry San Joaquin River channel to serve CVP exchange contractors.

longer reach spawning grounds. After a consortium led by the Natural Resources Defense Council (NRDC) sued and prevailed in the courts, a settlement agreement between the consortium and the Friant Water Users Authority led to restoration studies (with findings expected in 2002). The agreement adopted two guiding principles: that the river's natural functions be restored and that irrigators not lose water or additional money. In 2003, the issue returned to court when negotiations broke down.

# Colorado River Delivery Systems

The Colorado River is currently the source for up to 12 percent of California's developed water. Six other states along the river's watershed, plus the nation of Mexico, share allocated portions of the river's flow. (Map 16.) California's allotment is 4.4 million acre-feet per year. Three-fourths of that is used to irrigate 900,000 acres of farmland. Priority water rights are held by three irrigation districts. The Palo Verde Irrigation District (PVID) is located 110 miles north of the Mexican border, just west of the river. The Imperial Irrigation District (IID), in Imperial County, south of the Salton Sea, receives the majority of the state's Colorado River allotment via the All-American Canal. The Coachella Valley Water District (CVWD) serves farms north of the Salton Sea, in parts of Riverside, Imperial, and San Diego Counties (map 17.)

The fourth priority water right is held by the MWD. Member agencies of "the Met" include 14 cities, 12 municipal water districts, and one county water authority. It is the water wholesaler to 95 percent of the South Coast region. Along that coastal plain, from Ventura County down to the Mexican border, the MWD provides about 60 percent of the water supply. The Colorado River portion of its supply (SWP water also serves the MWD) travels 242 miles, crossing the desert in the Colorado River Aqueduct.

Lake Mead, behind Hoover Dam, is the primary storage reservoir in the lower Colorado River basin. The Colorado River Aqueduct begins at Parker Dam, 155 miles downstream from Hoover. The aqueduct can handle 1.2 million acre-feet annually, or more than 1 billion gallons a day. (Pls. 69, 70.)

The newest large reservoir in California was completed by the MWD in 1999. Diamond Valley Reservoir, near Hemet, was built to alleviate concerns that aqueducts feeding Southern California could be cut off by earthquakes and to provide optional water during droughts. The off-stream reservoir was filled in 2002 with 800,000 acre-feet of water (a six-month

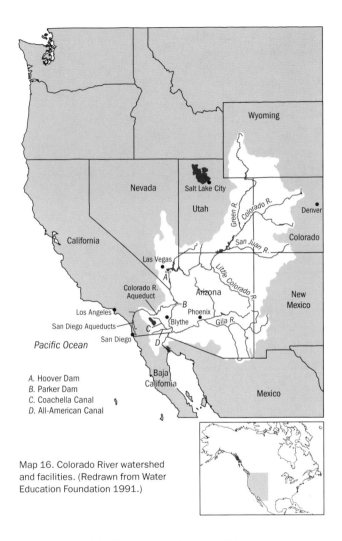

Map 16. Colorado River watershed and facilities. (Redrawn from Water Education Foundation 1991.)

A. Hoover Dam
B. Parker Dam
C. Coachella Canal
D. All-American Canal

supply for the MWD) from the Colorado River Aqueduct and the California Aqueduct.

Every drop of Colorado River water has been allocated to water rights holders. In fact, the river is overallocated, because

Plate 69. Parker Dam, which forms Lake Havasu, the diversion point for Colorado River water into the Colorado Aqueduct.

Plate 70. The Colorado River Aqueduct crossing the desert.

apportionments to the states were based on overestimates of the annual runoff. In *Cadillac Desert* (1986, 126), Marc Reisner described the Colorado as "unable to satisfy all the demands on it, so it is referred to as a 'deficit' river, as if the river were somehow at fault for its overuse." Of course, the Colorado is not to blame. The river itself is not a water rights holder.

In a treaty, the United States promised to pass along 1.5 million acre-feet of Colorado River water as far as the border

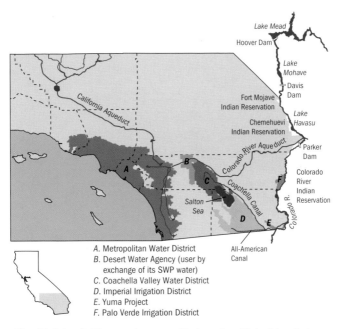

Map 17. Colorado River service areas. (Redrawn from Water Education Foundation 1991.)

Map labels:
Lake Mead
Hoover Dam
Lake Mohave
Davis Dam
Fort Mojave Indian Reservation
Chemehuevi Indian Reservation
Lake Havasu
California Aqueduct
Colorado River Aqueduct
Parker Dam
Coachella Canal
Colorado River Indian Reservation
Salton Sea
Colorado R.
All-American Canal

A. Metropolitan Water District
B. Desert Water Agency (user by exchange of its SWP water)
C. Coachella Valley Water District
D. Imperial Irrigation District
E. Yuma Project
F. Palo Verde Irrigation District

of Mexico. In most years, diversions inside Mexico have left nothing to reach the Gulf of Mexico. There was once a wetlands estuary at the mouth of the Colorado; the United States, Mexico, and the International Boundary and Water Commission are studying possibilities for restoring it.

For many years, California took more than its allocated 4.4 million acre-feet of Colorado River water, because other states in the lower river basin were not prepared to divert their full allotments. Southern Californians became accustomed to about 800,000 acre-feet of surplus to keep the MWD's Colorado River Aqueduct full; they took a total of 5.3 million acre-feet in 2000. But by then, Arizona had plumbing in place to handle all of its allotment, and Nevada, with the Las Vegas region booming, was asking to exceed its portion.

The secretary of the interior controls use of the river's "surplus" water. Under pressure from the other Colorado River states, the secretary ordered California to show good progress toward weaning itself from the extra 800,000 acre-feet or face mandatory cuts. The Colorado River Water Use Plan, or "4.4 Plan," was to be ready by December 31, 2002, and had to convince the other watershed states that it was realistic. Planners aimed to reallocate 800,000 acre-feet annually within Southern California without pulling more from Northern California's already heavily impacted rivers. That meant that Imperial and Coachella Valley agriculture had to give up water. The alternatives of urban demand reduction or population stabilization to live within the limits of the existing water supply were not given serious consideration.

A list prepared for the 4.4 Plan included a transfer of 110,000 acre-feet between the MWD and the IID, a transfer of 200,000 acre-feet between the IID and the San Diego County Water Authority (SDCWA), a shift of 100,000 acre-feet between the IID and the CVWD, the lining of irrigation canals with concrete to control seepage and save 94,000 acre-feet, and groundwater sources totaling 300,000 acre-feet in Arizona, the Mojave Desert, and the Coachella Valley.

There were problems with almost all of the proposals. Groundwater banking for future withdrawals was not as controversial as pumping of native groundwater. Conservation measures, such as concrete lining of irrigation canals, were not as controversial as land fallowing, which would shut down extended economies in farm communities. In the Imperial Valley, fallowing would also exacerbate the salinity issues of the Salton Sea, because irrigation flows to the sea would be cut back. The IID balked at land fallowing and wanted assurances that it would not be liable for damages to the Salton Sea environment.

When the deadline arrived with no agreement, the Department of the Interior announced it would immediately reduce the MWD's access to surplus water by about 415,000 acre-feet. It also intended to punish the IID by shifting about 200,000 acre-feet from the farmers to the MWD (though the overuse had all originated with the urban wholesaler). The IID vowed to legally fight the attack on its historic water rights, yet the forced transfer of agriculture water to serve urban interests seemed to be a sign of California's future.

## The Los Angeles Aqueduct

Completed in 1913, the Los Angeles Aqueduct brings water from the Eastern Sierra to the city of Los Angeles (map 18). Construction of this aqueduct and its associated reservoirs was the first major long-range water delivery project in California. The city acquired water rights by purchasing 300,000 acres of the Owens Valley, or about 98 percent of all the private land in that Eastern Sierra valley, hundreds of miles north of Los Angeles. The imperialistic pressure exerted by a distant city on unwilling rural landowners became an ugly part of California's water history. The aqueduct was extended into the Mono Basin and began diverting streams away from Mono Lake in 1941 (pls. 71, 72).

Plate 71. Lee Vining Creek at the point where water is diverted from the Mono Lake tributary into the Los Angeles Aqueduct.

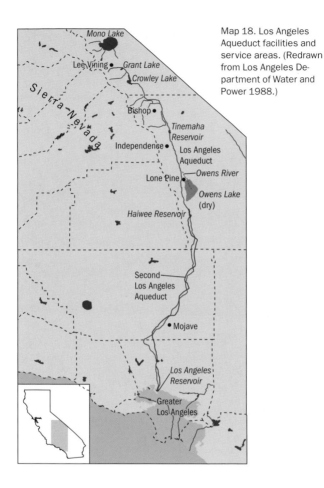

Map 18. Los Angeles Aqueduct facilities and service areas. (Redrawn from Los Angeles Department of Water and Power 1988.)

The Los Angeles Department of Water and Power moves an average of 400,000 acre-feet of Eastern Sierra water to the city each year—enough to serve about 3.2 million people. With additional MWD water and some local groundwater, the Los Angeles population has grown to four million, at least eight times the number that local water supplies would have allowed. (Pl. 73.) That growth is one of the clearest examples

Plate 72. Los Angeles Aqueduct pipe in the upper Owens Valley.

Plate 73. The cascade, visible from the Golden State Freeway, where Los Angeles Aqueduct water enters the San Fernando Valley.

of William Mulholland's observation "Whoever brings the water, brings the people." Mulholland was the engineer who oversaw the early design, construction, and operation of the Los Angeles Aqueduct system.

After four decades of stream diversions from the Mono Lake basin, damage to the lake and the dewatering of its tributary streams fostered an environmental battle in the 1980s and victory for the lake defenders in 1994. Other issues arose when dust from the bed of Owens Lake, which was completely dried up by the diversions, became a major air pollution source at the south end of the Owens Valley. To stabilize Mono Lake, correct violations of air quality laws, and rewater portions of the lower Owens River, Los Angeles has found ways to reduce its reliance on Eastern Sierra water. Most of that reduction has been achieved through water conservation. The city pursued an aggressive program of toilet replacement, offering free low-flush toilets to its customers. This and other conservation and water-recycling efforts allowed Los Angeles to grow by 30 percent during the final decades of the twentieth century, yet see a seven percent *decrease* in its total water use and a 15 percent drop in per capita demand.

## The Hetch Hetchy Aqueduct

The Hetch Hetchy Aqueduct brings Tuolumne River water to 2.3 million people in San Francisco and other portions of the Bay Area (map 19). The system originates at Hetch Hetchy

*Below and facing page:* Map 19. Hetch Hetchy Aqueduct, facilities, and service areas. (Redrawn from San Francisco Public Utilities Commission, no date.)

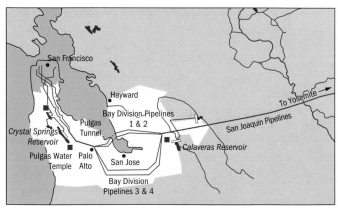

Valley, inside Yosemite National Park, where O'Shaughnessy Dam was completed in 1923 to dam the Tuolumne River (pls. 74, 75). The water system of the San Francisco Public Utilities Commission (SFPUC) also includes five reservoirs in the Bay Area: two in Alameda County (San Antonio and Calaveras) and three on the Peninsula south of San Francisco (San Andreas, Crystal Springs, and Pilarcitos). Those reservoirs supplement the system with runoff from local watersheds, but 85 percent of the city's water comes from the Tuolumne River. About two-thirds of that Hetch Hetchy water is sold to 26 other cities and water districts in San Mateo, Santa Clara, and Alameda Counties.

The system also generates electricity—a major revenue source for San Francisco (pl. 76). After water leaves Hetch Hetchy, it passes through tunnels leading down to a series of powerhouses. Three massive pipes then bring water across the Central Valley. The aqueduct that delivers water to San Francisco is entirely gravity fed, so a 25-mile-long tunnel had to be constructed through the Coast Ranges. One segment of the aqueduct crosses beneath the south part of the bay and another portion swings south of the bay. They rejoin at the Pulgas Water Temple, a monument marking the arrival point for aqueduct water on the Peninsula (pl. 77).

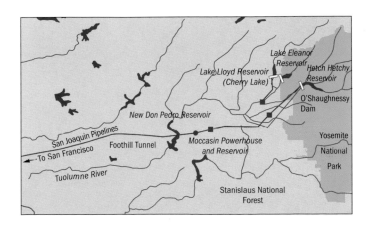

Plate 74. Hetch Hetchy Valley, 1913.

Plate 75. O'Shaughnessy Dam and Hetch Hetchy Reservoir, inside Yosemite National Park.

Some of the exceptionally clean Tuolumne water goes directly into the city's water system, and some is stored in the Peninsula reservoirs. Hetch Hetchy water that goes directly to city pipelines does not have to be filtered, because it exceeds

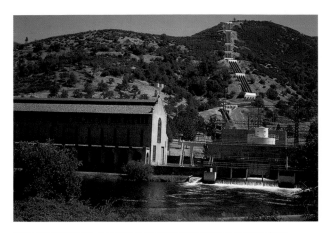

Plate 76. Moccasin, a hydroelectric power plant that is part of the SFPUC's Hetch Hetchy system.

water quality standards (it is disinfected with chlorine). Only a few cities in the nation are authorized to use unfiltered water.

Hetch Hetchy Valley, where that clean water is first stored, is about two-thirds the size of, and very similar in character to, the more famous Yosemite Valley. The Tuolumne River meandered through its meadows and trees, beneath towering granite cliffs and domes punctuated by waterfalls. The idea of building a dam inside a national park, and in that particular valley, infuriated John Muir. "These temple destroyers, devotees of ravaging commercialism, seem to have a perfect contempt for Nature, and, instead of lifting their eyes to the God of the mountains, lift them to the Almighty Dollar," Muir declared in 1912, as congressional hearings were about to start to consider the project. "Dam Hetch Hetchy? As well dam for water tanks the people's cathedrals and churches, for no holier temple has ever been consecrated by the heart of man" (1912, 181).

Muir argued that there were other rivers available to San Francisco, including the Mokelumne (which would be devel-

Plate 77. The dedication ceremony, in 1934, at the Pulgas Water Temple, above Crystal Springs Reservoir.

oped soon after for East Bay cities). Congress authorized the reservoir construction by passing the Raker Act in 1913. When President Woodrow Wilson signed the law, he stated that domestic water supply was the "highest use" of the river water, even though it originated in a national park.

Concerns about the old, deteriorating Hetch Hetchy Aqueduct system's ability to withstand earthquakes led to a $1.7 billion bond, approved by voters in the November 2002 election, to fund repairs and upgrades. Because two-thirds of the SFPUC's water customers had no say in its management decisions, some of their contracting agencies had also pushed for state legislation to require oversight of the repairs, and even for a new regional utility district something like the MWD to oversee water distributions.

Those who wanted to see the restoration of Hetch Hetchy Valley saw an additional possibility: that O'Shaughnessy Dam might actually be removed from Yosemite National Park. The Restore Hetch Hetchy organization proposed a project that would have developed alternative water storage as part of the capital improvement program and required no loss of water for San Francisco. They asked that a feasibility study be included in the bond proposal sent to the voters; that did not happen, but county supervisors did pass a resolution promising to (someday) consider the visionary proposal.

## The Mokelumne Aqueduct

"East Bay MUD" is the nickname for the East Bay Municipal Utility District, which serves 35 communities in Alameda and Contra Costa Counties, including Berkeley and Oakland, and parts of the San Ramon Valley (map 20). It is an earthy nickname for an agency that supplies domestic water to about 1.2 million people.

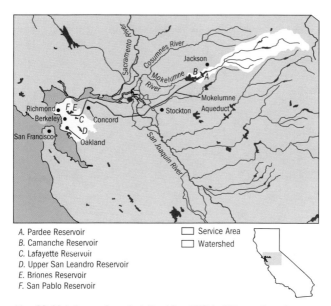

A. Pardee Reservoir
B. Camanche Reservoir
C. Lafayette Reservoir
D. Upper San Leandro Reservoir
E. Briones Reservoir
F. San Pablo Reservoir

☐ Service Area
☐ Watershed

Map 20. Mokelumne Aqueduct/East Bay MUD facilities and service areas. (Redrawn from Montgomery 1999.)

The Mokelumne River in the central Sierra Nevada is the source for virtually all of EBMUD's water. The watershed drains parts of Alpine, Amador, and Calaveras Counties. EBMUD built the Pardee Dam across the Mokelumne in the foothills northeast of Stockton. Pardee can hold a 10-month supply of water. Below Pardee is Camanche Reservoir, which helps regulate releases to serve downstream water rights holders and the fisheries and riparian habitat needs of the lower river.

EBMUD owns almost 30,000 acres in the Mokelumne River watershed and 25,000 acres of other watershed lands in the East Bay. After a 30- to 45-hour trip, water in the system has traveled 91.5 miles across the Central Valley via the Mokelumne and Lafayette Aqueducts to enter East Bay reservoirs or filter plants. Basins in the Berkeley and Oakland Hills contain the San Pablo, Briones, Lafayette, Upper San Leandro, and Chabot Reservoirs (pl. 78).

EBMUD also holds an American River entitlement that could be sent to the Mokelumne Aqueduct via the Folsom South Canal. This supplemental supply has only been tapped

Plate 78. EBMUD's San Pablo Reservoir, east of Tilden Regional Park.

once, during the drought year of 1977 to 1978, when it was actually pumped from the Delta. This intake point generated controversy. EBMUD preferred the cleaner water taken from the American River, but environmentalists and the city of Sacramento were concerned about the impacts of such diversions on the river. A decades-long legal battle led to affirmation of EBMUD's water right, but modifications have been negotiated. The intake point was shifted to just downstream from Sacramento, to maintain minimum flows in the American until it merges with the Sacramento River.

## The North Bay

Some cities north of San Francisco Bay, including Santa Rosa, Petaluma, San Rafael, and Mill Valley, are served by the Sonoma County Water Agency. Their primary water source is the Russian River, via the Santa Rosa, Sonoma, Petaluma, and North Marin Aqueducts and the Cotati Intertie. The agency also taps into the headwaters of the Eel River, diverting that water into the Russian River through a tunnel. The fast-growing cities of Vallejo, Fairfield, and Vacaville are served by the Solano County Water Agency, which captures Putah Creek water in Lake Berryessa and ships it south in the Putah South Canal. SWP water delivered by the North Bay Aqueduct adds to the Solano supply.

The state has thousands of water agencies and districts; 280 retail water agencies serve about 90 percent of California's users. The San Diego County Water Authority is an example of one of the intermediate layers in the water supply hierarchy. SDCWA is an MWD member that imports 84 percent of the county's water. It serves six cities, four rural water districts, three irrigation districts, eight municipal water districts, one public utility district, and a federal military base. The Colorado River provides 73 percent of its water; 27 percent comes from the SWP (both sources are delivered, of course, by the MWD). In addition to SDCWA supplies, the county also relies on local sources (including surface water, groundwater, recycled water, and some water produced by desalination) that make up 16 percent of the total mix.

With so many agencies and many layers of decision making, coordination (or the lack of it) can be an obstacle to wise management of the resource. A Regional Water Authority established, in 2001, by 21 agencies in the Sacramento region was a hopeful sign that joint-powers agreements might be established elsewhere.

Because water is essential for life, every natural habitat and everything that lives in California has been affected by the redistribution of the state's water. (See table 3 for one way to look at this redistribution.) The aqueduct systems have fostered economic development and population growth. They have also generated a long list of challenges for Californians to face as they shape their future.

| Agency (headquarters location) | Annual Entit-lement, AF | 2002 Alloca-tions, AF (%) |
|---|---|---|
| **Upper Feather River** | | |
| Butte County, Board of Supervisors (Oroville) | 3,500 | 1,575 (45) |
| Plumas County FC&WCD (Quincy) | 1,630 | 865 (53) |
| Yuba City, Public Works (Yuba City) | 9,600 | 4,320 (45) |
| **North Bay Area** | | |
| Napa County FC&WCD* (Napa) | 21,100 | 9,495 (45) |
| Solano County Water Agency (Vacaville) | 46,296 | 20,833 (45) |
| **South Bay Area** | | |
| Alameda County FC&WCD* Zone 7 (Pleasanton) | 78,000 | 35,100 (45) |
| Alameda County Water District (Fremont) | 42,000 | 18,900 (45) |
| Santa Clara Valley Water District (San Jose) | 100,000 | 45,000 (45) |
| **San Joaquin Valley** | | |
| Castaic Lake Water Agency | 12,700 | 5,715 (45) |
| Dudley Ridge Water District (Fresno) | 57,343 | 25,804 (45) |
| Empire/West Side Irrigation District (Stratford) | 3,000 | 723 (24) |
| Kern County Water Agency (Bakersfield) | 1,000,949 | 450,427 (45) |
| Kings County (Hanford) | 4,000 | 1,800 (45) |
| Oak Flat Water District (Westley) | 5,700 | 2,565 (45) |
| Tulare Lake Basin Water Storage District (Corcoran) | 111,527 | 50,187 (45) |
| **Central Coast** | | |
| San Luis Obispo County FC&WCD* (San Luis Obispo) | 25,000 | 11,250 (45) |
| Santa Barbara County FC&WCD* (Santa Barbara) | 45,486 | 20,469 (45) |
| **Southern California** | | |
| Antelope Valley/East Kern Water Agency (Quartz Hill) | 141,400 | 63,630 (45) |
| Castaic Lake Water Agency (Santa Clarita) | 82,500 | 37,125 (45) |
| Coachella Valley Water District (Coachella) | 23,100 | 10,395 (45) |
| Crestline/Lake Arrowhead Water Agency (Crestline) | 5,800 | 2,610 (45) |

*continued* ➤

**TABLE 2.** *continued*

| Agency (headquarters location) | Annual Entit-lement, AF | 2002 Alloca-tions, AF (%) |
|---|---|---|
| Desert Water Agency (Palm Springs) | 38,100 | 17,145 (45) |
| Littlerock Creek Irrigation District (Littlerock) | 2,300 | 1,035 (45) |
| Metropolitan Water Dist. of S. California (Los Angeles) | 2,011,500 | 905,175 (45) |
| Mojave Water Agency (Apple Valley) | 75,800 | 34,110 (45) |
| Palmdale Water District (Palmdale) | 21,300 | 9,585 (45) |
| San Bernardino Valley MWD (San Bernardino) | 102,600 | 46,170 (45) |
| San Gabriel Valley MWD (Azusa) | 28,800 | 12,960 (45) |
| San Gorgonio Pass Water Agency (Beaumont) | 4,000 | 1,800 (45) |
| Ventura County Flood Control District (Ventura) | 20,000 | 9,000 (45) |
| **Total State Water Project Entitlements/Allocations** | **4,125,031** | **1,855,768 (45)** |
| (Over the years, SWP deliveries have averaged 2.3 million acre-feet) | | |

*FC&WCD = Flood Control and Water Conservation District.
Source: Compiled from Department of Water Resources reports.

## TABLE 3. Where Does Your Water Come From?

Sources: **1.** Groundwater; **2.** Feather River/California Aqueduct/State Water Project; **3.** Colorado River/Metropolitan Water District of Southern California*; **4.** Owens and Mono Basins/Los Angeles Aqueduct/L.A. Department Water & Power; **5.** Tuolumne River/San Francisco PUC; **6.** Mokelumne River/East Bay Municipal Utility District; **7.** Russian and Eel Rivers/Sonoma County Water Agency; **8.** Lake Berryessa/Putah Creek/Solano County Water Agency; **9.** Central Valley Project (many Northern California rivers)/U.S. Bureau of Reclamation; **10.** local reservoirs/streams; **11.** ocean desalination

Agoura Hills 2, 3, 10
Alameda 6, 10
Albany 5, 10
American Canyon 2
Anaheim 1, 2, 3
Antioch 9, 10
Apple Valley 1*†
Arcadia 1, 2, 3
Arcata 10
Arroyo Grande 1, 10
Artesia 1, 2, 3, 10
Atascadero 1
Atwater 1
Auburn 10
Avenal 9
Azusa 1, 2, 3
Bakersfield 1, 2, 10
Baldwin Park 1, 2, 3
Banning 1
Barstow 1
Bell 1, 2, 3
Bell Gardens 1, 2, 3
Bellflower 1, 2, 3
Belmont 5, 10
Benicia 2, 10
Berkeley 6, 10
Beverly Hills 2, 3
Blythe 1, 10
Brawley 3
Brea 1, 2, 3
Buena Park 1, 2, 3
Burbank 1, 2, 3
Burlingame 5
Calabasas 2
Calexico 3
Camarillo 1, 2

Campbell 1, 2, 9, 10
Canyon Lake 1, 3, 10
Carlsbad 2, 3
Carpinteria 1, 2, 10
Carson 1, 2, 3
Cathedral City 1
Ceres 1
Cerritos 1, 2, 3
Chico 1
Chino 1, 2
Chino Hills 1, 2, 3
Chula Vista 2, 3, 10
Claremont 1, 2, 3
Clearlake 10
Clovis 1
Coachella 1
Colton 1*†
Commerce 1, 2, 3
Compton 1, 2, 3
Concord 9, 10
Corona 1, 2, 3, 10
Coronado 2, 3, 10
Costa Mesa 1, 2, 3
Covina 1, 2, 3, 10
Cudahy 1, 2, 3
Culver City 1, 2, 3
Cupertino 1, 2, 5, 9, 10
Cypress 1, 2, 3
Daly City 1, 5, 10
Dana Point 2, 3
Davis 1 (UC Davis 2, 8)
Delano 1
Diamond Bar 2, 3
Dinuba 1
Dixon 1
Downey 1, 2, 3

Duarte 1
Dublin 1, 2, 10
East Palo Alto 5, 10
El Cajon 2, 3, 10
El Centro 3
El Cerrito 6, 10
El Monte 1, 2, 3
El Segundo 2, 3
Encinitas 2, 3, 10
Escondido 2, 3, 10
Eureka 10
Fairfield 2, 8
Fillmore 1
Folsom 9
Fontana 1, 2, 10
Foster City 5
Fountain Valley 1, 2, 3
Fremont 1, 2, 5
Fresno 1, 9
Fullerton 1, 2, 3
Galt 1
Garden Grove 1, 2, 3
Gardena 1, 2, 3
Gilroy 1
Glendale 1, 2, 3
Glendora 1, 2, 3
Grand Terrace 1*†, 2
Grover Beach 1, 10
Hanford 1
Hawaiian Gardens 1, 2, 3
Hawthorne 1, 2, 3
Hayward 5, 6, 10
Hemet 1, 2, 3, 10

*continued* ➤

**TABLE 3.** *Continued*

Hercules 6, 10
Hermosa Beach 1, 2, 3
Hesperia 1*†
Highland 1, 2, 10
Hillsborough 5, 10
Hollister 1
Huntington Beach 1, 2, 3
Huntington Park 1, 2, 3
Imperial Beach 2, 3, 10
Indio 1
Inglewood 1, 2, 3
Irvine 1, 2, 3
La Canada Flintridge 1, 2, 3, 10
La Habra 1, 2, 3
La Mesa 2, 3, 10
La Mirada 1, 2, 3
La Palma 1, 2, 3
La Puente 1, 2, 3
La Quinta 1
La Verne 1, 2, 3
Lafayette 6, 10
Laguna Beach 2, 3
Laguna Hills 2, 3
Lake Elsinore 1, 3, 10
Lake Forest 2, 3
Lakewood 1, 2, 3
Lancaster 1, 2
Larkspur 7, 10
Lawndale 1, 2, 3
Lemon Grove 2, 3, 10
Lemoore 1
Livermore 1, 2, 10
Lodi 1
Loma Linda 1*†
Lomita 1, 2, 3
Lompoc 1
Long Beach 1, 2, 3
Los Alamitos 1, 2, 3
Los Altos 1, 2
Los Angeles 1, 2, 3, 4
Los Banos 1
Los Gatos 1, 2, 9, 10

Lynwood 1, 2, 3
Madera 1
Manhattan Beach 1, 2, 3
Manteca 1
Marina 1, 11
Martinez 9
Marysville 1
Maywood 1, 2, 3
Menlo Park 5, 10
Merced 1
Mill Valley 7, 10
Milpitas 2, 5, 9
Mission Viejo 2, 3
Modesto 1
Monrovia 1, 2, 3
Montclair 1, 2
Montebello 1, 2, 3
Monterey 1, 10
Monterey Park 1, 2
Moorpark 1, 2
Moraga 6, 10
Moreno Valley 1, 2
Morgan Hill 1
Mountain View 1, 2, 5, 9, 10
Murrieta 1, 2, 3, 10
Napa 2, 10
National City 1, 2, 3, 10
Newark 1, 2, 5
Newport Beach 1, 2, 3
Norco 1
Norwalk 1, 2, 3
Novato 7, 10
Oakdale 1
Oakland 6, 10
Oceanside 1, 2, 3, 11
Ontario 1, 2, 3
Orange 1, 2, 3
Orinda 6, 10
Oroville 1, 2, 10
Oxnard 1, 2
Pacific Grove, 1, 10
Pacifica 5

Palm Desert 1
Palm Springs 1, 10*†‡
Palmdale 1, 2, 10
Palo Alto 5
Palos Verdes Est. 2, 3
Paradise, 10
Paramount 1, 2, 3
Pasadena 1, 2, 3, 10
Paso Robles 1
Perris 2, 3
Petaluma 7
Pico Rivera 1
Piedmont 6, 10
Pinole 6, 10
Pittsburg 1, 9
Placentia 1, 2, 3
Pleasant Hill 6, 9
Pleasanton 1, 2, 10
Pomona 1, 2, 10
Port Hueneme 1
Porterville 1
Poway 2, 3, 10
Rancho Cucamonga 1, 2, 10
Rancho Mirage 1
Rancho Palos Verdes 2, 3
Red Bluff 1
Redlands 1, 2, 10
Redondo Beach 1, 2, 3
Reedley 1
Rialto 1, 2, 10
Richmond 6, 10
Ridgecrest 1
Riverbank 1
Riverside 1*§
Rocklin 10
Rohnert Park 1, 7
Rosemead 1, 2, 3
Roseville 9
Sacramento 1, 9, 10
Salinas 1, 10
San Anselmo 7, 10
San Bernardino 1*†, 2, 10

**TABLE 3.** *Continued*

San Bruno 1, 5, 10
San Carlos 5
San Clemente 1, 2, 3
San Diego 2, 3, 10
San Dimas 1, 2, 3
San Fernando 1, 2
San Francisco 5, 10
San Gabriel 1, 2, 3
San Jacinto 1, 2, 10
San Jose 1, 2, 5, 9, 10
San Juan Capistrano
   1, 2, 3
San Leandro 6, 10
San Luis Obispo 1, 2,
   10
San Marcos 2, 3
San Marino 1, 2, 3
San Mateo 5, 10
San Pablo 6, 10
San Rafael 7, 10
San Ramon 6, 10
Sanger 1
Santa Ana 1, 2, 3
Santa Barbara 1, 2,
   10, 11
Santa Clara 1, 2, 5, 9,
   10
Santa Clarita 1, 2
Santa Cruz 1, 10
Santa Fe Springs 1, 2,
   3
Santa Maria 1, 2, 10

Santa Monica 1, 2, 3
Santa Paula 1, 10
Santa Rosa 7, 10
Santee 2, 3
Saratoga 10
Seal Beach 1, 2, 3
Seaside 1, 10
Selma, 1
Shafter 1
Sierra Madre 1, 10
Simi Valley 1, 2
Soledad 1
South El Monte 1, 2, 3
South Gate 1, 2, 3
South Lake Tahoe 1,
   10
South Pasadena 1, 2,
   3
South San Francisco 1,
   5
Stanton 1, 2, 3
Stockton 1, 10
Suisun City 2, 8
Sunnyvale 1, 2, 5, 9,
   10
Susanville 1, 10
Temecula 1, 2, 3, 10
Temple City 1, 2, 3
Thousand Oaks 2
Torrance 1, 2, 3
Tracy 1, 9
Truckee 1

Tulare 1
Turlock 1
Tustin 1, 2, 3
Twentynine Palms 1
Ukiah 1
Union City 1, 2, 5
Upland 1, 2, 10
Vacaville 1, 2, 8
Vallejo 2, 8, 10
Ventura 1, 10
Victorville 1*†
Visalia 1
Vista 1, 2, 3, 10
Walnut 2, 3
Walnut Creek 6, 9
Wasco 1
Watsonville 1
West Covina 1, 2, 3, 10
West Hollywoo, (east)
   4; (west) 2, 3
West Sacramento 1, 9,
   10
Westminster 1, 2, 3
Whittier 1
Windsor 1, 7
Woodland 1
Yorba Linda 1, 2, 3
Yuba City 1, 2, 10
Yucaipa 1, 2, 10
Yucca Valley 1*†

* MWD is also the largest customer for SWP water.

† Groundwater is replenished with State Water Project water.

‡ Riverside uses 99.9% groundwater; the rest is MWD's blend of SWP and Colorado River water.

§ Palm Springs groundwater is replenished with Colorado River water in exchange for SWP allotment.

Source: Water Education Foundation 1994 and numerous water district sources. Cities listed have populations greater than 10, 000.

STAY OUT OF AQUEDUCT
QUEDENSE FUERA DEL ACUEDUCTO
YOU MAY DROWN
SE PUEDEN AHOGAR

DANGER
PELIGRO

SWIFT COLD WATER
AGUA SUMAMENTE FRIA
STEEP SLIPPERY BANKS
BANCOS ALTOS Y RESBALOSOS
EXIT LADDERS EVERY 1,000 FT.
ESCALERAS DE SALIDA CADA 1,000 PIES

*Historically, water development in California may have had more of an impact on biodiversity than any other single factor.*

—ANDREW COHEN, *LIFE ON THE EDGE*

*Each of us has had a toxic waste hauler dumping surreptitiously into the groundwater for us by proxy. We may not do this ourselves, but we willingly participate in a system that fosters such destruction.*

—ARTHUR VERSLUIS, "WATERS UNDER THE EARTH"

# Extinction Is Forever

Ninety-five percent of California's original wetlands and 89 percent of its riparian woodlands are gone. About 1,400 dams in California convert flowing rivers and streams into reservoirs; in the Sierra Nevada, 600 river-miles have been flooded. (Map 21.) It is no coincidence that California is also the state with the most endangered and threatened species.

Water development and changes in the waterscape are responsible for California's distinction as one of the globe's extinction epicenters of the twentieth century. Dams store water supply, generate electricity, and help control flooding. They also destroy many of the natural processes of rivers and river ecosystems, not just where a reservoir pools water, but also downstream. Dams trap sediments, depriving beaches along the river and on the coast of sand. Without sediment deposits and periodic high flows, riparian vegetation is lost, spawning gravels are not maintained, and habitat diminishes for everything in the food chain supported by river ecosystems.

Dams kill fish inside spinning turbines or when fish screens are ineffective at points of diversion. They also change water temperatures downstream. If dams release surface waters that are much warmer than natural flows, fish may become more susceptible to diseases. Some dams send colder-than-normal, oxygen-depleted water downstream from the bottoms of reservoirs. The native fish of the Colorado River adapted to spring floods that provided warm, nutrient-rich waters for spawning. Releases from Colorado River dams, however, are now clear and cold. Inherent in flood control by dams is modification of natural river fluctuations; peak flows are reduced, and that water is stored for release during dry seasons. Flooding's beneficial effects—scouring sediments, replenishing spawning gravels, and fertilizing floodplains—are lost. Another primary function of most dams is to enable water diversions. Despite state laws that require that enough water remain in streams, after diversions, to protect fisheries

Map 21. California dams. (Redrawn from California Dams Database, no date.)

Plate 79. Salmon leaping.

and public trust values, some rivers have been completely dewatered, and most have too little water.

Freshwater entering the ocean used to be characterized as "a worthless loss." Salmon and other anadromous fish would undoubtedly disagree. They make return trips to inland spawning grounds by tracking the chemical signatures of the river waters of their birthplace as those waters blend into the ocean. Nearly every river or stream that reached the coast of California once supported runs of salmon, Steelhead Trout *(Oncorhynchus mykiss)*, or Pacific Lamprey *(Entosphenus tridentatus):* fish born in freshwater that migrated to the ocean and returned to spawn. California's four distinct runs of Chinook Salmon *(Oncorhynchus tshawytscha),* also called King Salmon, are named according to the timing of their passage through the Delta as they return from the sea. Winter-run Chinook come back to spawn after one to three years in the ocean. Spring-run adults are most often three years old; unlike those in the other runs, they do not mate and die immediately, but spend the summer high in the watershed, where the water stays cool, and then spawn in late August and September. Fall-run Chinook come in two waves, early and late fall, after spending one to three years in the ocean (pl. 79).

Coho Salmon *(Oncorhynchus kisutch),* also called Silver Salmon, were once abundant in 582 coastal streams from Monterey Bay up to the Oregon border. Steelhead once used almost every stream along the coast of California. (Steelhead are Rainbow Trout that have gone to sea—genetically identical, it appears, to the rainbows that live their lives in freshwater streams.)

Californians may wonder why so much media attention has been devoted to these fish in recent years. Why is water for salmon considered particularly important? Or water for another anadromous fish, the tiny Delta Smelt *(Hypomesus transpacificus)*? That two-to-three-inch-long fish was once one of the most common in the Sacramento–San Joaquin Delta estuary. Smelt spend their adult lives in the interface zone where salt and freshwater mix, and move upstream into freshwater to spawn. They are particularly dependent on flows entering the estuary, flows that have been greatly reduced by diversions above and within the Delta. The small fish are also very susceptible to "entrainment," being sucked into diversion pumps. Delta Smelt were listed as threatened under the Endangered Species Act in 1993. When large concentrations of smelt came near, pumps had to be shut down. Stopping the pumps reduced supply reliability and water quality for water providers who depended on Delta diversions.

The salmon and Steelhead decline has been more noticeably dramatic. Millions once migrated up California's rivers and streams. They were "keystone species" in the rivers, and their loss became one measure of the greater loss of wildlife and riparian habitat in California. In the winter of 1883 to 1884, over 700,000 salmon were caught for commercial sale along the Delta. In that era, voracious canneries depleted the vast salmon populations, but it was the dams constructed during the 1940s, 1950s, and 1960s that dealt the near-fatal blow to the species. The Sierra Nevada Ecosystem Project, a 1996 study for Congress, found that only about 676 miles of stream habitat for salmon remained accessible, of 1,774 miles once used in the Central Valley and Sierra Nevada. More crit-

ical than lost stream length was the inability to reach spawning sites in the upper reaches of those streams; only 10 percent
of suitable spawning habitat remains. (Map 22.)

In the Sacramento River system just 191 winter-run Chinook returned in 1991. Spring-run numbers were down to
2,300 in 1992. The winter-run has been listed as endangered
and the spring-run as threatened. Fall-run Chinook are the
only salmon that now are present in both the Sacramento and
the San Joaquin watersheds; this run is also threatened. Coho
Salmon, estimated at one million in the mid-1800s, num-
bered less than 6,000 in coastal streams in 1996. The population south of San Francisco Bay is endangered. Other genetically distinct Coho populations in Northern and Central
California are threatened. Steelhead Trout are classed as endangered along the South Coast. Genetically distinct populations on the Central and North Coasts are threatened.

Salmon are amazing water creatures. Born in our rivers,
they mature in the ocean and return to their birthplace to re-
produce. During their time offshore, they may travel more
than 2,000 miles across the ocean; some reach the coast of
Siberia. As each returns toward its home estuary, it somehow
detects the "fingerprint" scent of *the* river that it must follow
back to its birthplace. Salmon noses can detect the identify-
ing substances in concentrations as low as one part per
3,000,000,000,000,000,000!

After entering the river, salmon stop feeding. Their entire
metabolism develops "tunnel vision," focused on traveling and
the ultimate reproductive goal. Their digestive tracts break
down. Stored fat and muscle are converted to energy to power
their upstream battle against the current. They run a gantlet
of predators, including bears, osprey, and, for thousands of
years, Native American fishermen. They leap over cascades
and physical obstacles. If they successfully pass a dam by nav-
igating a fish ladder, they may still become confused by the
slack water of a reservoir, because the push upriver, against a
current, is part of their genetic hardwiring.

A female that reaches her home destination looks for clean

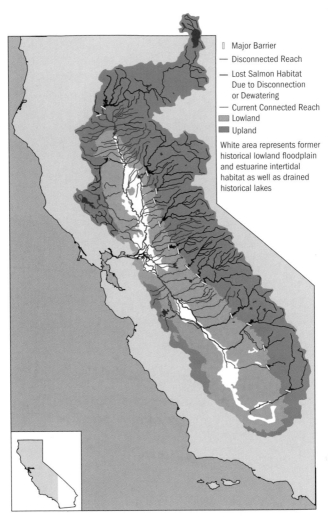

Legend:

⏹ Major Barrier
— Disconnected Reach
— Lost Salmon Habitat Due to Disconnection or Dewatering
— Current Connected Reach
▨ Lowland
▨ Upland

White area represents former historical lowland floodplain and estuarine intertidal habitat as well as drained historical lakes

Map 22. Disconnected salmon rivers. (Redrawn from Bay Institute of San Francisco 1998.)

gravel with a flow of oxygenated water passing through. She digs a nest and releases hundreds of eggs while a nearby male fertilizes them. Somehow, as gametes fuse, the new life records the chemical signature of the home water. When parent fish are intercepted during migration and taken to a hatchery on another creek, their offspring, raised in chemically different water, return to the hatchery creek rather than follow the traditional route.

Parents die soon after spawning. Their large decomposing carcasses serve as food for their offspring and for many insects, other fish, mammals, and birds. The great biomass of salmon flesh is essential to many species along the river. Fry that emerge from eggs may spend more than a year in the home stream or head immediately downstream for the sea, depending on the species. They need unpolluted, cool water that is shaded by riparian vegetation. Many of the insects that salmon eat in the river also depend on willows, cottonwoods, and similar shoreline plants to complete their life cycles. Young smolt pass the same gantlet of predators and barriers that their parents ran in reverse. As they finally reach salt water, they undergo physical adaptations to the ocean.

As dams and diversion canals were planned and constructed, the obstacles they presented to fish *were* anticipated. Fish screens were designed to fend fish off from the diversion intakes to canals (pl. 80). Fish ladders were constructed, and hatcheries were built (pl. 81). The California Department of Fish and Game operates eight salmon and Steelhead hatcheries, and the U.S. Fish and Wildlife Service operates two hatcheries in California (map 23). Although these efforts are well intentioned and of some benefit, the declining numbers of fish have made apparent the ineffectiveness of many of the older fish screens, ladders, and hatcheries. What the migrating fish need most is an adequate share of free-flowing water.

That lesson was suggested at Butte Creek, one of the Sacramento River tributaries. In 1987, a drought year, only 14 Chinook Salmon returned to spawn there. Although many fac-

*Above:* Plate 80. Colusa fish screen, in 1972. It was redesigned in 1998 to decrease fish mortality. Here Sacramento River water is diverted into the Glenn-Colusa Canal.

*Right:* Plate 81. Salmon being sorted for artificial spawning at the Feather River Fish Hatchery.

Map 23. California fish hatcheries. (Redrawn from California Department of Fish and Game, no date.)

tors can influence the success of a salmon run, in 1988, the year after small dams along Butte Creek were removed, 20,000 Chinook made it to the spawning grounds.

Conflicts between water for fish and water for farms generated a public outcry during the summer of 2001 on the border between Oregon and California. The U.S. Bureau of Reclamation, faced with a drought and needing to maintain minimum flows in the Klamath River to protect endangered species of fish, told farmers they had to cut irrigation water by 90 percent. "Dreams Dry Up in Klamath Basin," the *Los Angeles Times* headline read on July 23. The story called "the unfolding tragedy…the culmination of a century of unsustainable federal policies designed to satisfy demands for cropland, fishing, population growth and wildlife protection." The human issue was more complex than just "farmers versus fish." A major fishing and canning industry for *other* humans, on the coast, depended on the Klamath River salmon runs. The fish had also been the cultural lifeblood and dietary staple of Hoopa and Yurok Indians living along the river.

Overallocation of the Klamath River system had parallels to the problems of the San Joaquin and Colorado River systems, where consequences of unrealistic water allocations and unsustainable population growth were being realized. The reason Californians were "suddenly" hearing so much about salmon and smelt, water conflicts and endangered species, as the twentieth century closed was that resources had been stretched far beyond natural limits. (Pl. 82.)

The Endangered Species Act is societal recognition that human actions should not cause any species to disappear forever from the Earth. Enforcement of habitat protection measures that follow listing under the act can be controversial and feel onerous to people whose activities are affected. But enforcing the act requires ending the threat. Other laws also protect water-dependent species, but lack of effective enforcement (often due to underfunding) has been a problem in California's water management.

Four of the tributary streams feeding Mono Lake were completely dried by diversion into the Los Angeles Aqueduct. Section 5937 of the state Fish and Game Code, adopted in 1937, read, in part, "The owner of any dam shall allow sufficient water at all times to pass through a fishway, or in the absence of a fishway, allow sufficient water to pass over, around,

Plate 82. A close-up look at salmon at the Nimbus Fish Hatchery during the American River Salmon Festival.

or through the dam, to keep in good condition any fish that may be planted or exist below the dam." That is a mandatory law: it uses the word "shall," rather than "may." Court tests have affirmed that the law applies to all dams, regardless of when they were approved or constructed.

Correcting violations of this law was part of the environmental victory at Mono Lake that in 1994 produced a protective plan approved by the State Water Resources Control Board. In 1995, the SWRCB also affirmed, in *California Trout, Inc. v. Big Bear Municipal Water District*, that "the protection of fisheries from inadequate flows is necessary regardless of where fish live, be it in the largest navigable river or the smallest mountain stream." That ruling stated, "Fish were granted that protective right the instant California became a state in the Union."

Although a half million spring-run Chinook migrated up the San Joaquin River each year before Friant Dam was built by the CVP, about 60 miles of the San Joaquin were dewatered after 1942. Efforts to correct that violation of state law are under way. Meanwhile, portions of every stream in the Tulare Basin remain dry, the water running elsewhere through pipes and irrigation canals. The express purpose of Pine Flat Dam, on the Kings River, was to keep water from ever reaching its traditional terminus in Tulare Lake, so crops could be grown on the dry lakebed.

## A Thirsty Garden

Each of us eats more than 4,500 gallons of water per day in our food, according to the California Farm Bureau. California is the number one agricultural state in the nation, with nine of the top 10 agricultural counties in the United States. Agriculture contributes $20 billion each year to the state's economy. Of all the country's produce, 55 percent is grown here, and

Plate 83. "Food Grows Where Water Flows."

California is the nearly exclusive source of special crops such as almonds, artichokes, dates, figs, olives, and raisins. (Pl. 83.)

In California, land and water rights held by farmers have historically made agricultural property attractive to urban developers. Los Angeles County was the leading agricultural county in the nation until the 1950s. The Santa Clara Valley, today's fully urbanized "Silicon Valley," was also once a major producer of fruits and vegetables. Repeating the pattern, the Central Valley is now under heavy pressure from urban sprawl. Every year, 15,000 acres of agricultural land in the state succumb to concrete and asphalt. Farms are also being pulled out of production when urban suppliers purchase agricultural water.

Across California, nine million acres of farmland rely on irrigation water. With 80 percent of the state's developed water going to agriculture, and urban interests ever thirsty, how well farmers conserve their portion is a major concern. Water availability defines options for crops and irrigation methods. Grapes grown with drip irrigation may use one to two feet of water on each acre (pl. 84). Cotton, grown in the same location with flooded furrows, requires three to four acre-feet. Much of the water used by agriculture in the state goes to five crops: alfalfa, cotton, rice, grapes, and irrigated pasture. Pres-

Plate 84. Drip irrigation of grapes.

Plate 85. Orchard irrigation with groundwater pumping.

surized drip and microspray systems are efficient and work well for some crops but are not as effective on others. Overirrigation can put runoff water, with salts, fertilizers, and pesticides, into groundwater basins and surface water. (Pls. 85, 86.)

California is a major rice-growing state. Though rice fields must be flooded, rice actually takes less water to grow *per serving* than almost any other crop in the

Plate 86. Vegetable crops flood irrigated with siphon tubes from a canal.

Plate 87. Flooded California rice fields.

state. Rice fields also substitute for some of the lost wetlands habitat in the Central Valley, benefiting migratory waterfowl. (Pl. 87.)

That kind of environmental mitigation was not always the norm. The standard "reclamation" practices of the nineteenth and early twentieth centuries aimed primarily to convert "worthless" mosquito-infested wetlands into productive farmland. Agricultural expansion was behind many of the habitat losses in California. Agriculture also became a major contributor to water pollution in the state's surface and groundwater ecosystems. Yet, for 20 years, farmers in California were exempted from Clean Water Act controls on insecticides, herbicides, and other pollutants that entered the state's waters. One dormant-spray pesticide, Diazinon, used in Central Valley almond orchards, began reaching San Francisco Bay during high-runoff episodes in concentrations over 100 times the allowable limits. The agricultural waiver was to end in 2002, as the SWRCB planned to issue the first statewide "general permit" controlling irrigation return waters and stormwater runoff from farms.

Crops separate irrigation water from most of the salts it carries, leaving the minerals concentrated in the soil. To keep salination from increasing to the point where no plant can survive, farmers must apply more water than the plants need. The extra water flushes salts down into the groundwater below. In many places soil overlies impermeable layers, so the excess water and salts cannot drain away. When they accumulate and reach back into the root zone, farming may become impossible. Around the world, including in the Fertile Crescent of the Middle East, salination has been the historic bane of irrigated agriculture.

Different crops have different tolerances for soil salinity. Strawberries are very sensitive. Cotton, alfalfa, pomegranates, and pistachios are salt-tolerant commercial crops. Some plants, such as eucalyptus trees, actually "mine" salts. The Westlands Water District planted eucalyptus trees at the edges of fields to absorb salty drainage water, with limited success. The district, on the west side of the southern San Joaquin Valley, has some of the greatest salinity problems in California. That side of the valley has soils created by marine sediments that were naturally saline. An extensive clay layer below the topsoil also blocks deep percolation of irrigation water. On the east side of the valley, by contrast, granitic soils drain well and are naturally low in mineral salts.

Water sources used for irrigation vary in their salinity. The Sacramento River carries about 270 pounds of salts in each acre-foot, compared to 2,000 pounds in the Colorado River. The diminished flows of the lower San Joaquin River carry 1,200 pounds per acre-foot (and up to 3,300 pounds at times); a total of 1.3 million tons of salt annually enters the Delta from the San Joaquin River.

To drain off saline waters, farmers bury perforated pipes, called tiling, at spaced intervals beneath fields. Sometimes the runoff gathered this way goes into flowing rivers and the ocean. In other places it goes to local evaporation ponds. (Pl. 88.)

The San Joaquin Valley's drainage problems were anticipated when the CVP was designed. The San Luis Drain was planned to carry water northward through the valley all the way to Suisun Bay. Eighty-five miles of the drain were built, beginning in the south. By 1973, the drain reached as far as

*Above:* Plate 88. A drainage canal for returned agricultural water in the San Joaquin Valley.

*Left:* Plates 89a and 89b. Black-neck Stilt *(Himantopus mexicanus)* embryos, normal (S-313) and deformed, from a Kesterson Reservoir nest (S-9), in 1985.

Kesterson National Wildlife Refuge, near Gustine. Concerns about the impacts of sending the polluted water into the Delta halted construction, forcing the water to remain at Kesterson. In 1983, after a decade of drainage water ponding there, thousands of waterfowl and shorebirds began to be born with deformities and to die. Bird embryos had protruding brains, missing eyes, twisted bills, and grossly deformed legs and wings (pl. 89). Elevated selenium levels were responsible.

Selenium is a trace element found in the soils on the west

side of the San Joaquin Valley. It is necessary for life but, in a process called biomagnification, can become concentrated to toxic levels as it ascends a food chain. Not just birds were affected; toxic levels of the substance showed up in insects, frogs, snakes, and mammals (concentrated selenium can also be toxic to humans). The drain to Kesterson was closed in 1986. Selenium in farm runoff and evaporation ponds across the state has been closely controlled since that time.

A drainage solution had been promised to farmers receiving CVP water, however, and court decisions confirmed that some solution must be provided. The ultimate solution probably will not be a Delta outflow, where salts would impact water headed for so many domestic users. Another option, sending drainage water directly westward to the ocean, could cause major environmental impacts on the Monterey Bay National Marine Sanctuary. So the Westlands Water District began negotiating a 200,000-acre federal buyout of its most impacted lands.

Even without the contributions of the San Luis Drain, San Joaquin River flows that approach the Delta today consist of little but agricultural drainage water. The Regional Water Quality Control Board (RWQCB) enforces Total Maximum Daily Load (TMDL) requirements for contaminants in the state's waters. A TMDL specifies the maximum amount of a pollutant that a water body can receive before being declared impaired or polluted, and allocates pollutant "loadings" among point and nonpoint sources. Tougher discharge standards for the San Joaquin must be complied with soon by those CVP exchange contractors whose water supply out of the Delta is saltier than the water that originally flowed to them out of the mountains, down the San Joaquin.

With discharge standards tightening, "Grassland Area" farms, on the west side of the San Joaquin Valley near Los Banos, initiated a regional drainage effort for 97,000 acres. Their goal became finding ways to keep from delivering any salty water to the San Joaquin River. With tiling in place beneath about 30,000 acres by 2002, subsurface water was collected and used to irrigate salt-tolerant crops. Asparagus, alfalfa, pistachios, pomegranates, and Bermuda grass were grown. Salts, inevitably, will continue to concentrate. After several decades, the farmers will have to deal with permanent storage of very concentrated slurries.

Farther south, on the former bed of Tulare Lake, from which no rivers drain, 44,000 farm acres have constant salinity issues. Tilewater is gathered and delivered to 4,700 acres of evaporation ponds. Unfortunately, as at Kesterson, such ponds look quite attractive to birds. The law now requires that evaporation ponds be designed to discourage use by birds (with steep walls and frightening sounds and calls). Nearby alternative wetlands and nesting habitats, with features meant to *attract* birds, are maintained with clean water.

## The Salton Sea

Imperial Valley drainage issues present a particular dilemma in the southern desert. In this valley, 38,000 miles of subsurface drainage pipes gather water from 500,000 irrigated acres. The Salton Sea is the "evaporation pond" for that water, taking in more than four million tons of dissolved salt and tens of thousands of tons of fertilizers each year. It is now 25 percent saltier than the ocean. Yet 400 million fish still reside in its harsh water, making it the most productive fishery in the United States.

As wetland habitat disappeared from Southern California's coast, the Salton Sea became an essential alternative site for millions of migratory birds—a critical rest and feeding spot along the Pacific Flyway. Bird tagging has revealed that Salton Sea birds fly everywhere across North America. Almost the entire population of Eared Grebes *(Podiceps nigricollis)* in North America uses the sea, and it serves endangered species such as the Brown Pelican *(Peleicanus occidentalis)*, Yuma Clapper Rail *(Rallus longirostris)*, Black Rail *(Laterallus jamaicensis)*, and Greater Sandhill Crane *(Grus canadensis)*. Birds take ad-

Plate 90. The Salton Sea, teeming with life but a place of disturbing mortality.

Plate 91. The bones from tilapia die-offs covering the beach at the Salton Sea.

vantage of the sea's enormous productivity. The food chain begins with algae fertilized by farm runoff nutrients. Hot-weather algae blooms, however, lead to algae mortality and decomposition that can consume more oxygen than photosynthesis generates. Oxygen-depleted water then causes fish to suffocate. Fish die-offs may be responsible for an assortment of diseases and death in bird populations. Though it still teems with life, paradoxically, the changing sea is also a place of widespread, disturbing mortality (pls. 90, 91).

Furthermore, salinity levels are approaching the limits for any fish. If no freshwater entered to replace evaporation, the sea could lose its fish in two to 11 years. It takes about 1.5 million acre-feet to replace evaporation off the sea each year. Should less water enter, the sea would decline and rapidly concentrate the salts it already contains. To stabilize the salinity level would require not only enough farm runoff to replace evaporated water, but removal of four million tons of salt sent to the sea from Imperial Valley farms each year.

Exacerbating efforts to address the Salton Sea's progressive salination, coastal cities have plans to purchase water from Imperial Valley farmers to service more population growth and development. Although the farm drainage water gradually increases salinity in the Salton Sea, losing Colorado River water to those cities would cause a more rapid decline in water level and further concentration of the salts.

The Salton Sea has sometimes been dismissed as a "man-made mistake." Yet the below–sea level basin flooded many times in the past, whenever the Colorado River shifted its course that direction. The physical size of the sea means it will not simply stop drawing migratory birds. Allowing it to completely dry up would leave birds with even less habitat in a state that has paved over most of its wetlands. Drying up the sea would also expose a vast source of fine particulate dust, creating air pollution problems far greater than those at Owens Lake. Dust clouds off the lakebed would have multi-county impacts.

Imperial Valley farming, though incredibly productive in a climate that allows multiple harvests each year, is sometimes dismissed as a waste of water in that desert environment. About half the land in Imperial Valley grows alfalfa, a crop that uses twice as much irrigation water there as in other parts of the state. If up to 25 percent of the farmland were to be fallowed, as has been suggested, Colorado River water not used on that acreage *could* be allocated directly to the Salton Sea. That kind of decision, a water right directly tied to the environment, would signal a major change of public attitude and of water law in California.

# Animal Impacts

Agricultural runoff comes not solely from farm fields growing plant crops. California has 40 million acres of rangelands for grazing livestock, lands that are drained by 9,000 miles of waterways. Cattle love to hang out in the shade offered by trees that line streams and ponds, and they also like to stay close to drinking water. Their urine and feces accumulate there and introduce nitrates that promote algae growth. The ammonia in the urine is toxic to many aquatic creatures. Concentration of cattle near water also has other consequences for water quality. Where riparian vegetation is eaten away or trampled, shade is reduced and water temperatures can become too high for fish. Streambanks may also become unstable. Destabilized streams can form deep cuts that drain groundwater out of nearby meadows. Overgrazing of a watershed can increase runoff and lead to flooding that carries sediments into water sources. Ranchers can minimize these effects by fencing cattle out of streams and riparian areas and alternating short-duration, intense grazing with rest periods.

Dairies and feedlots, where cattle are confined instead of freely grazing across pastures or rangelands, generate enormous concentrations of waste. Contrary to the cute images in television ads that promote California's dairy products, most modern dairies do not allow their cows to wander idyllic pastures (pl. 92). The Chino Basin, in Riverside and San Bernardino Counties, on the upper watershed of the Santa Ana River, has the highest concentration of dairies anywhere in the world, with 300 facilities holding up to 40 cows per acre. Each of those 325,000 cows produces 22 tons of waste in a year, totaling enough to cover a football field eight stories

Plate 92. Up to her knees in muck; the polluted water must be properly managed by dairy farmers.

Plate 93. A waste "lagoon" for gathering fertilizer and urine runoff from a dairy in the Santa Ana River watershed.

higher than the Empire State Building! The Central Valley is another dairy center, where over 800,000 cows in 1,600 dairies generate as much waste every year as 30 million people.

Cow urine and feces contain ammonia and nitrates and other salts that must be kept out of water supplies. The SWRCB and the nine RWQCBs require dairies to isolate watering and feeding areas from streams and to divert rainfall runoff away from manure areas. They are also supposed to recycle manure, urine, and the water used to hose down facilities, storing it in leak-proof lagoons until it is used to irrigate and fertilize pastures. Lagoons have been known to leak or overflow, however, when not well designed and maintained. They constantly release noxious gases. To avoid polluting streams or groundwater, manure from the lagoons has to be applied to fields no faster than crops can absorb it. (Pl. 93.)

## Beneath Your Feet

We cannot know all of the bad news hidden beneath our feet, the product of our casual disregard or mistaken belief that the ground could clean anything. As we have learned, actual cleaning of contaminated aquifers is costly and difficult. Some contamination is impossible to correct; only time, measured in centuries, may bring a solution. The city of Fresno learned that bitter lesson when 50 of its 300 domestic wells were contaminated by a pesticide and had to be closed.

Industrial and mining contamination reflect water's natural talents as a solvent. Some of the pollution has been with us since the gold rush or before. Mercury was widely used by 49ers and the miners who followed them to separate gold from ore. The toxin is still present in Gold Country rivers. Hardrock mines came later; today, drainage water emerges from many of them as strong as battery acid (pl. 94). Arsenic, a naturally occurring carcinogen, made national news when the Clinton administration adopted more stringent drinking-water standards that the Bush administration first set aside, then later adopted.

Other contaminants are as modern as rockets and the atomic bomb. Radioactive slag heaps from uranium mines in the Colorado River Basin above Lake Mead threaten that water supply for Southern California. Perchlorate, a rocket fuel that affects thyroid glands, is moving in underground plumes that may take thousands of years to reach discharge areas. The En-

Plate 94. Acidic mine drainage in the Sacramento River headwaters.

vironmental Protection Agency (EPA) announced, in July 2001, a 240-year "restoration plan" for groundwater contaminated with perchlorate from an Aerojet site near Rancho Cordova. The Sacramento suburb has nine wells with undrinkable water and 13 others at risk from the spreading plume. Perchlorate plumes in Arizona threaten the Colorado River. Perchlorate contamination from a Lockheed plant affects groundwater wells in Rialto, Mentone, Loma Linda, Redlands, and Riverside, all in Riverside County.

There are numerous other examples of industrial groundwater pollutants. The State Department of Health Services identified 37 wells (out of 246 tested) in the San Gabriel Valley that were contaminated with an industrial solvent, trichloroethylene (TCE), also used by Aerojet. Chromium-6 forced the city of Glendale to stop using groundwater for half of its supply and switch solely to surface water sources. The movie *Erin Brockovich*, about a groundwater contamination lawsuit against Pacific Gas & Electric over chromium-6 used in a power plant, broadened public awareness of the health issues and consequences of such contamination.

Methyl tertiary butyl ether (MTBE) is a gasoline additive that was intended to reduce air pollution by improving fuel efficiency. It has an incredible affinity for water, easily dissolves, and spreads into groundwater wherever fuel tanks leak. (Pl. 95.) MTBE is a carcinogen that gives water an unpleasant turpentine smell and taste. Boat engines introduce it into reservoirs and lakes. Anyone who has ever looked closely at the water near a marina where boats operate has seen gasoline and oil scum mirroring the surface. The two-stroke carbureted engines of jet skis, or "personal watercraft," are notorious for their inefficiency; such engines dump a gallon of gasoline directly into the water for every five gallons burned (pl. 96). In 2001, all two-stroke engines (not just jet skis) were banned at Lake Tahoe and at Whiskeytown National Recreation Area. By the end of 2003, all MTBE was to be phased out and replaced by ethanol as a fuel efficiency additive in gasoline in California.

# Out of Sight, Out of Control

The California Constitution stipulates that water is owned by the people and must not be wasted or put to an unreasonable use by those who have water rights. Beyond that overall requirement, groundwater, unlike surface water, is not under statewide control. Historian Norris Hundley Jr. has characterized California's approach to groundwater "management" as a "chaotic and environmentally destructive practice of management by numerous local water districts and agencies—a practice that has meant no management at all" (2001, 530). (Map 24.)

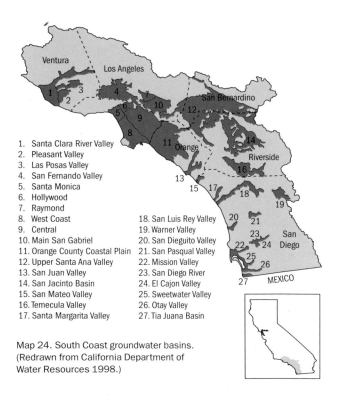

1. Santa Clara River Valley
2. Pleasant Valley
3. Las Posas Valley
4. San Fernando Valley
5. Santa Monica
6. Hollywood
7. Raymond
8. West Coast
9. Central
10. Main San Gabriel
11. Orange County Coastal Plain
12. Upper Santa Ana Valley
13. San Juan Valley
14. San Jacinto Basin
15. San Mateo Valley
16. Temecula Valley
17. Santa Margarita Valley
18. San Luis Rey Valley
19. Warner Valley
20. San Dieguito Valley
21. San Pasqual Valley
22. Mission Valley
23. San Diego River
24. El Cajon Valley
25. Sweetwater Valley
26. Otay Valley
27. Tia Juana Basin

Map 24. South Coast groundwater basins.
(Redrawn from California Department of
Water Resources 1998.)

Plate 95. Water-filled excavations marking where leaky gas tanks must be replaced. Decontaminating the groundwater itself is far more difficult.

Plate 96. A jet ski. Some jet skis can dump a gallon of gasoline into the water for every five gallons burned.

A clear example occurred as urban sprawl spread out of Southern California's coastal basin into the Mojave Desert. The Mojave River groundwater basin produces a net annual supply of 50,900 acre-feet, but the pumping rights of basin landowners total 280,000 acre-feet. Priority rights go to those who acquired land first. Meanwhile, every new resident in the sprawling developments exacerbates the problem, because with land ownership comes the right to pump groundwater. A first plan, submitted during adjudication of the overallocated, overdrafted groundwater basin, did not get court approval.

The 1998 California Water Plan, prepared by DWR, identified a statewide groundwater overdraft of 1.5 million acre-feet and forecast increased losses, particularly from the Tulare Lake and San Joaquin basins. This overdraft, figured into the supply and demand water budget of the plan, made up the bulk of the state's overall supply shortage, which has averaged about 2.2 million acre-feet per year.

Overdrafting can lead to land subsidence. As groundwater extraction empties the pores between particles, fine-grained sediments are compacted. Subsidence generally does not mean that the aquifer cannot later be recharged. Though fine-

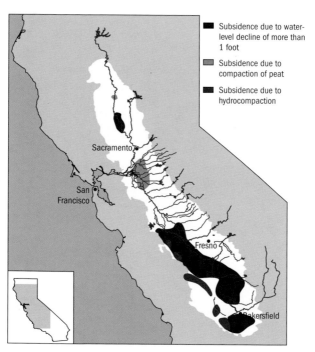

Map 25. Central Valley land subsidence. (Redrawn from Williams, Prudic, and Swain 1969.)

Plate 97. Near Mendota, in the San Joaquin Valley. The land subsided nearly 30 feet here due to groundwater pumping between 1925 and 1977.

grained sediment compaction is often not reversible, most of the storage capacity of aquifers is not in such fine material, but in coarser sediments. Land subsidence is primarily a threat to roads, buildings, canals, and low-lying coastal areas that may be flooded by seawater. Overpumping in Santa Clara County in the 1930s caused the ground beneath San Jose to sink so far that it was threatened with flooding during high tides in San Francisco Bay. When the South Bay Aqueduct came on line in 1965, the local water district purchased water from the SWP to reduce groundwater dependence. (Map 25.)

Subsidence was a great problem in the first half of the twentieth century. Correcting San Joaquin Valley overdrafting became a primary purpose of the CVP. (Pl. 97.) Subsidence became noticeable again during the drought of 1987 to 1993, when farmers increased their groundwater pumping.

Parts of the San Joaquin Valley dropped eight feet. At Edwards Air Force Base, where the space shuttle lands on the desert side of the mountains north of Los Angeles, subsidence caused 12-foot-deep, 2,000-foot-long fissures on a runway.

Groundwater pumping can also lead to seawater intrusion. As in the Bay-Delta, where river flows hold back surface salt water, removing freshwater from the water table may allow salt water to intrude far inland through the ground. In the Salinas Valley, seawater moved six miles inland into a 180-foot-deep aquifer and two miles inland into a 400-foot-deep aquifer. Orange County began percolating water in settling basins and injecting it through wells back in the 1950s, once Colorado River water imports were available. This and other coastal water districts successfully created hydraulic barriers to block seawater from contaminating domestic water supply wells.

## Can You Drink the Water?

Water agencies generally follow six steps to clean their water supply before sending it to domestic users: aeration, spraying as in a fountain to release gases; coagulation, to cause fine particles to join together; flocculation, which mixes sediments so they combine and settle out; sedimentation in quiet basins, which can remove about 85 percent of suspended matter; filtration through coal, sand, and gravel; and disinfection.

We add small amounts of poisons to our water to kill microbes and control infectious diseases. For decades the most common disinfectant used was chlorine. Chlorination has saved millions of lives by reducing the incidence of typhoid fever, cholera, and other diseases spread by water. Unfortunately, it can also produce carcinogenic and mutagenic by-products. Water providers seek to assess and balance these risks. To control human exposure, the EPA sets standards for disinfectants and their by-products, and the SWRCB and RWQCBs enforce them.

Overexposure can cause eye, nose, and stomach discomfort (chlorine and chloramines); nervous system effects (chlorine and chlorite); and, in infants and young children, anemia (chlorine and chlorite). Cancer risks are associated with other disinfectant by-products, such as bromate, haloacetic acids, and trihalomethanes (THMs). THMs also cause liver, kidney, and central nervous system disorders. THMs form in chlorinated waters that contain high concentrations of dissolved organic compounds and bromide. This is a big issue in the Sacramento–San Joaquin Delta, where the estuary naturally generates lots of organic material, while seawater delivers the bromide.

Joe Thornton, in *Pandora's Poison: Chlorine, Health, and a New Environmental Strategy,* summarized epidemiological evidence supporting a link between THMs and human cancers. One New Jersey Department of Health study

> found that exposure to total [THMs] in drinking water was associated with reduced birthweight, fetal growth retardation, and malformations of the heart, oral cleft, and nervous system.
>
> And a very large, well-designed study by the California Department of Health Services found that the risk of spontaneous abortion is 80 percent higher among women who drank five or more glasses of chlorinated tapwater with relatively high THM levels during pregnancy than among women with lower exposures. The association was apparent at THM concentrations well below the maximum legal level in U.S. drinking water. (2000, 139)

Approximately 30 percent of U.S. drinking-water utilities have shifted to disinfecting with chloramines, containing chlorine and ammonia, which have fewer toxic by-products than chlorine alone. The long-term answer can be a shift to alternate technologies, which also eliminate accidental chlorine spills during transport and handling. Slow sand filtration mimics the natural filtering of groundwater, creating an "ecosystem" of tiny organisms that consume organic matter and disease-causing microbes. Ultraviolet radiation controls microbes by damaging their DNA and is cheaper than chlorine. Ozonation takes advantage of a powerful oxidant, ozone, that breaks down bacteria, viruses, pathogens, and organic compounds. It is expensive and also can produce some THMs. EBMUD uses ozonation at two of its water-processing plants, however. It has shown that, as long as an adequate dose of ozone is supplied, ozonation causes no measurable increase in the mutagenic activity of water.

## Giardia

One of the greatest pleasures of hiking in the Sierra Nevada used to be drinking directly from the clean mountain streams. Then, in the final decades of the twentieth century, came warnings about *Giardia lamblia,* apparently a threat in every stream and lake in the mountain range. Backpackers began boiling their water, lugging heavy bottles along the trails, or carrying special filter pumps or iodine disinfectants (pl. 98).

*Giardia* is the most commonly diagnosed intestinal parasite in North America. It is the most frequently identified cause of diarrheal outbreaks associated with drinking water in this country; the Centers for Disease Control (CDC) estimates that as many as 2.5 million cases occur annually. Studies have shown that 10 or so cysts are

Plate 98. Filtering water in the backcountry to minimize the risk of *Giardia.*

required to create a reasonable probability of contracting giardiasis; about one-third of persons ingesting 10 to 25 cysts pass detectable cysts in their stools.

In 1984, the U.S. Geological Survey (USGS) and the California Department of Public Health examined 69 Sierra Nevada streams, two-thirds of which were considered to have a high probability of human fecal contamination. *Giardia* cysts were found at 43 percent of the high-use sites and at 19 percent of the low-use sites, but always at very low concentrations. The highest concentration was 0.108 cysts per liter of water in Susie Lake, south of Lake Tahoe. The next highest was 0.037 per liter near Long Lake, southwest of Bishop. Samples taken in the Mount Whitney area varied from zero, at most sites, to 0.013 in Lone Pine Creek.

By comparison, San Francisco city water, renowned for cleanliness that allows it to be delivered unfiltered, can contain 0.12 cysts per liter, a higher concentration than that measured anywhere in the Sierra. Los Angeles Aqueduct water, with only 0.03 cysts per liter, has a higher concentration than all but two of the sites surveyed in the Sierra.

Robert Rockwell, who summarized these data on *Giardia* for a 2002 article that questioned widespread concerns about backcountry water, concluded that good backpacker hygiene combined with commonsense choices about where to pull drinking water from streams (upstream from trails, away from camps, in good flows with plenty of aeration) may be far more important in avoiding giardiasis than treating or filtering water. "Better safe than sorry" may be the philosophy that dictates water treatment, despite these findings.

# Mass Medication

Community water fluoridation has been endorsed by the American Dental Association, the American Medical Association, the American Association of Public Health, the U.S.

Public Health Service, the CDC, and the World Health Organization. Since 1997, California state law has required fluoridation by all communities with populations greater than 10,000 (so long as they have outside funding, rather than tax money, to install and operate the systems). About one-third of Californians drink fluoridated water. With both expert and legal backing, it might seem sensible to medicate all of the population this way. Yet voters in the cities of Redding, Santa Barbara, Santa Cruz, Modesto, and Watsonville have rejected proposals to fluoridate their water supplies. What is a common citizen to think about vocal opposition whenever a community considers this step?

Since the 1950s, several generations have been brought up hearing commercials for fluoride toothpastes that told them the chemical was good for them. Yet the fine print on tubes covered with cartoon characters reads: "WARNING: As with all fluoride toothpastes, keep out of the reach of children under six years of age. If you accidentally swallow more than used for brushing, seek professional assistance or contact a Poison Control Center immediately." Cautionary messages also warn doctors and parents not to give fluoride supplements to infants under the age of three or to pregnant women. Too much fluoride intake can rob bones of calcium, making them weak and brittle. Mottled teeth are an early symptom of fluorosis.

Part of this debate has centered on the argument that direct applications to teeth by dentists are more effective than systemic ingestion of the fluoride. Questions about efficiency and unintentional effects have also arisen; only seven percent of residential water is used for drinking, so 93 percent of the fluoride never "sees" a tooth before it washes down some drain in water cycling back to the environment.

Fluoride accidentally released in high concentrations into rivers has caused delayed salmon migrations, deformed embryos in salmon and trout, and accelerated mortality rates. The sodium fluoride used in water supplies is an EPA-listed hazardous waste product of the phosphate fertilizer industry. In concentrations far higher than those allowed in drinking water, it is poisonous and is used to kill insects and rats. It is the toxic element in the nerve gas Sarin.

Of course, many helpful substances are toxic at high concentrations. The control of overall dosage is the key to safe use. The standard fluoride dose, one part per million, is based on estimates of average daily water consumption, but dosage control, when the medicine is dispersed in drinking water, is nearly impossible. Fluoride is now in bottled juice and beer, on vegetables, and in every other product made or processed with fluoridated water.

Domestic water systems in Europe remain 98 percent fluoride free. Low cavity rates there are apparently related to improved standards of living, less eating of refined sugar, regular dental checkups, flossing, and frequent brushing.

Dentists, health providers, and lawmakers who promote fluoridation are obviously well intentioned. Some argue that the water supply is the only way that the poor will receive fluoride applications. This is a debate that revolves around society's willingness to solve one problem without creating others along the way.

## The Bottled-Water Phenomenon

Public concerns about tap water quality were partly responsible for the tripling of bottled-water sales in the 1990s. People are willing to spend from 240 to over 10,000 times more per gallon for bottled water than they typically do for tap water. At supermarkets, the cheapest bottled water sells for about a penny an ounce. Fancy imported bottles of water cost up to nine or 10 cents per ounce. The great majority is sold at two or three cents per ounce. At that average price range, one gallon of water costs between $2.90 and $5.30, and each acre-foot grosses from $945,000 to $1.7 million for retailers! By comparison, the MWD charges about $400 per acre-foot. Are buyers getting their money's worth? In particular, are they buying water that is purer than what comes out of their taps? (Pl. 99.)

Almost universally, labels on bottled water picture mountain snow, glaciers, or springs that emerge from the ground in a pristine, natural setting. The messages are of "purity" that comes from "nature." But bottled water is not necessarily cleaner or safer than most tap water. The Natural Resources Defense Council tested more than 1,000 bottles of 103 brands

Plate 99. The bottled water phenomenon is a sign of consumers' mistrust of tap water.

of bottled water for contaminants, and summarized its findings in a March 1999 petition to Congress asking the Food and Drug Administration (FDA) to better control the industry. About one-third of the waters tested contained levels of contamination that exceeded allowable limits.

Bottled water has to be tested, but it is sampled less frequently than city tap water for bacteria and chemical contaminants. Current standards for bottled water allow some (minute) contamination by *Escherichia coli* or fecal coliform, although *no* such contamination is allowable in tap water. And unlike tap water, bottled water is not required to be disinfected or tested for *Cryptosporidium* or *Giardia* parasites.

Amazingly, the NRDC found that about one-fourth of bottled water was nothing but tap water. Labels that read "from a municipal source" or "from a community water system" indicate that the water, however scenic its label, originated as tap water. Some, but not all, of those brands provide additional filtering or treatment. FDA rules allow bottlers to call their products "spring water," suggesting a natural source emerging from the ground, even though the water is extracted with pumps and then treated with disinfectants. The NRDC reported one label that read "spring water," with a picture of a lake surrounded by mountains, on bottled water that originated from an industrial parking lot next to a hazardous waste site.

The bottled-water phenomenon is an expensive and disturbing reaction by consumers, despite repeated assurances from water providers that their products are safe and clean. Recently the MWD discovered that Mexican-American immigrants were the state's biggest consumers of bottled water. Raised in a land where tap water was dangerous, they did not trust domestic drinking-water sources here. Despite our potable water standards and higher level of treatment, the contamination situation is disturbing and leads to mistrust among other consumers as well.

# The Problem Is Us

Clean water, like clean air, ought to be our birthright. That was the point of the Clean Water Act (CWA) of 1972, which was passed "to restore and maintain the chemical, physical, and biological integrity of the nation's waters." States were required to develop lists of impaired waters, rank those waters, and develop TMDLs for each source. The SWRCB and the EPA shared responsibility for enforcement in California. The first focus was on easily identifiable point sources, such as large factories and power plants. Nonpoint sources, the millions of impacts on water quality that are integral to our daily life, were a more intractable challenge.

The scope of the nonpoint-source problem became apparent when the USGS issued the results of a 2002 study of 139 streams in 30 states, including 10 in California. In those streams, they found a soup of products that are very familiar to the 34 million residents of this state, including antibiotics, ibuprofen and other painkillers, antacids, codeine, contraceptive hormones, perfumes, fire retardants, and caffeine. The USGS found the Sacramento River, just south of the capital city, to contain "higher levels of acetaminophen (the active ingredient in Tylenol), birth-control hormones and cholesterol than most waterways tested" across the nation. The message in these findings for human health, and for the rest of the life forms dependent on water habitats, is not yet known.

Another message is being sent from our beaches. In 2001, from Memorial Day through Labor Day, 613 health warnings were posted to close Orange County beaches and harbors. Bacteria levels were too high for swimmers and surfers. Those that ignored the warnings risked gastrointestinal problems; eye, ear, nose, and throat infections; and even hepatitis. (Pl. 100.)

Part of the problem is the number of people living in the coastal watersheds. Another part is the covering of up to 80 percent of the urban landscape with impervious surfaces, including buildings and roads, so that rainwater instantly runs off instead of settling into the ground. Most runoff entering storm drains is never treated. It carries pollutants from suburban yards into gutters and drains and then, typically, into water channels draining to the sea. Though San Francisco Bay is ringed by heavy industry, up to 70 percent of the pollutants entering the bay may originate from city streets and gardens. Urban dwellers have become familiar with stenciled messages like "Drains to the Ocean" on sidewalks above gutters, and with information campaigns that tell them, "You Are the Solution to Stormwater Pollution." Those are cautionary reminders about our connections to local watersheds and the greater water cycle (pl. 101).

Waste that actually receives some treatment may be responsible for part of the problem along Orange County's beaches. Sanitation districts in Orange County and San Diego have had federal waivers allowing them to pump sewage several miles offshore after only primary treatment. The waivers will not likely be extended. Evidence suggests that a massive

Plate 100. Closure notice at the Doheny State Beach lagoon in summer 2001.

Plate 101. "Drains to Bay" message discouraging dumping of oil and other pollutants into the storm drain.

plume of contaminated water accumulated at the Orange County sewage outfall and may have circulated back toward the beaches. The working theory had been that cold ocean water would "cap" the warmer layer where the sewage was being dumped, holding the plume in place. But studies by the University of California at Irvine and Scripps Institute of Oceanography suggested that circulation patterns were more complex and could possibly return sewage toward the shore. Christopher Evans, executive director of the Surfrider Foundation, made a good point in a *Los Angeles Times* story (May 17, 2002): "To argue about whether we should be dumping

240 million gallons of partially treated sewage in the ocean…
is goofy in the extreme."

# Where Does Your Dog Go?

You may diligently control your trash and oil and pesticide
use. Do you as diligently control your dog? We would never
think to defecate on the ground, wherever we might be when
the need arises, but many of us allow our pets to do so without
giving any thought to the consequences. Most people pick up
after their pets in their own yards, but many dogs roam (despite leash laws), and many dogs are taken for walks specifi-
cally to move the problem out of backyards. Then there are
outdoor cats, tidily burying wastes out of sight. The issue of
pet sanitation and polluted water has remained invisible to
most people, another example of how Californians ignore the
impacts of their own unending population growth. As the
human population increases, so do the numbers of our "fel-
low travelers," beloved dogs, cats, and other pets, all generating wastes every day.

The American Pet Products Manufacturers Association's
annual National Pet Owners Survey estimates that four in 10
(or 40 million) U.S. households own at least one dog. The average owner has about two dogs (1.7). With about 34 million
people in California, a formula developed for veterinarians to
estimate market statistics generates an estimate of 6.9 million
dogs and 7.7 million cats in the state. They are concentrated
where their human owners are concentrated, in the urban
centers, particularly along the Southern California and San
Francisco Bay coastal areas.

As much as 95 percent of the fecal coliform in urban
stormwater, in some studies, had a nonhuman origin. A Seattle study found that nearly 20 percent of the stormwater bacteria came from dogs. Dog feces can be a significant source of
fecal coliform and fecal strep bacteria. Dogs are also hosts of

*Giardia* and salmonella. Another study, published in July 2002, suggested that runoff to the ocean may be introducing a parasitic infection, toxoplasmosis, responsible for the deaths of sea otters. Domestic cats were the only animal group known to pass along the eggs of that parasite.

Proper cleanup and disposal are essential habits. The street gutter is the wrong place for feces disposal. Pet population control is another important part of the equation (as is human population stabilization, for that matter).

# Unchecked Growth: Messing with the Cycle

The biggest concern of California water planners remains the demand on water supply resulting from population growth in California. The 1998 California Water Plan projected that water demand would increase 38 percent in the next 20 years, while overall supply would only be augmented by 1.25 percent.

Some forces driving economic and population growth in recent decades have exacerbated water consumption. Silicon Valley (pl. 102), the concentration of high-tech industry at the south end of San Francisco Bay, could also be called "Thirsty Dotcom." Computer memory chips are made by etching circuit patterns, using acids and solvents, onto silicon wafers, which are then cut into many chips. Thousands of gallons of ultrapure water are used to rinse off the chemicals. Washing a single eight-inch silicon wafer uses about 2,000 gallons of water. Silicon Valley electronics firms collectively use millions of gallons of water each day.

The scale of human activities in California has become so massive that this state alone plays a significant role in global warming. California's 34 million people represent 0.5 percent of the Earth's population, yet we account for two percent of the fossil fuel burned as we generate over 400 million tons of

$CO_2$ a year (according to the California Energy Commission). As global carbon dioxide levels have increased, global warming has increased proportionately since 1900.

Scientists have now reached a broad, international consensus that global warming results from human activities. As increased levels of $CO_2$ and other "greenhouse gases" in the atmosphere trap solar energy, both global temperatures and climates are altered. The editor of *Science*, Don Kennedy, wrote (in the March 30, 2001, issue), "By now scientific consensus on global warming is so strong that it leaves little room for the defensive assertions that keep emerging from the cleverly labeled industrial consortium [of fossil fuel companies, automakers and energy utilities] called the Global Climate Coalition and from a shrinking coterie of scientific skeptics."

The conclusions are based on data from ice cores, tree rings, spring snow covers (which have decreased by 10 percent in the Northern Hemisphere), and the melting and collapse of polar ice. The sea level rose about 10 times faster during the twentieth century than during the last 3,000 years. Mountain glaciers are retreating; some of the Sierra Nevada's small glaciers are disappearing. El Niño events appear to be occurring more frequently. An increase in stream runoff during fall and winter has been documented, and the runoff traditional in April through July has decreased. Plant and animal species, including the Edith's Checkerspot Butterfly *(Euphydryas editha)*, have shifted their ranges northward and toward higher elevations, following the temperature and water conditions they need.

Californians may experience average annual temperature rises of three to four degrees F in the coming century, with winters five to six degrees warmer and summers one to two degrees warmer. Warmer temperatures will increase winter precipitation, but more of it may fall as rain and less as snow. The snowpack "reservoir" may diminish, while reservoir storage behind dams fails to meet the demand and winter floods increase. Should the sea level rise eight to 12 inches, it would

Plate 102. Santa Clara Valley, once a major agricultural region and now better known as Silicon Valley, its growth made possible by imported water.

take an additional 700,000 acre-feet of freshwater flowing through the Bay-Delta to offset saltwater intrusion. Islands that are now below sea level in the Delta, protected by levees, may be inundated.

Predictions about climate and water supply are not inevitable outcomes. As with population projections, which can become self-fulfilling when used to justify unending development, our society has a habit of extending graph lines outward and proclaiming *that* vision of the future as certain. Our own behaviors can alter these trends, particularly if we adopt aggressive measures to minimize the changes and impacts.

We face a daunting list of challenges. Yet the future is in our hands. Each of these water issues can be successfully addressed.

# MEETING THE CHALLENGES
## California's Water Future

*Watershed consciousness is…knowing where your water comes from…and where it goes when you flush, what happens to the rain that runs off your roof, what soils your home and community rest upon, and who shares your water supply.*

—PETER WARSHALL, *STREAMING WISDOM*

*The government tells us we need flood control and comes to straighten the creek in our pasture. The engineer on the job tells us the creek is now able to carry off more flood water, but in the process we have lost our old willows where the owl hooted on a winter night and under which the cows switched flies in the noon shade. We lost the little marshy spot where our fringed gentians bloomed.*

—ALDO LEOPOLD, *A SAND COUNTY ALMANAC*

# The Public Trust

The future of California water management will be guided by our laws. All water within California is owned by the state on behalf of the people. Since 1928, the California Constitution has required that water be put to the highest beneficial use; through most of the twentieth century that was interpreted as domestic or profit-making uses. The constitution also prohibits waste or unreasonable uses.

One of the first legal decisions to regulate impacts from water use came in 1884, when hydraulic miners were ordered to keep their waste-laden runoff confined on their own property so it would no longer damage property owners downstream. In 1931, as a reaction to Los Angeles's taking of Owens Valley water, "county of origin" provisions were written into the California Water Code to assure that water exports never deprived the county where the precipitation fell of water needed for its future development. Later, as the federal Central Valley Project began, "watershed of origin" provisions were added to the code to protect the "beneficial needs of the watershed, area, or any of the inhabitants or property owners therein" as the first priority, ahead of either federal or state export projects. In 1937, the Fish and Game Law to protect fisheries in streams below dams or diversions was enacted.

The 1970s brought passage of several major environmental protection laws, in reaction to degradation and losses that had been accelerating since World War II. In that decade, the federal Clean Water Act and Safe Drinking Water Act, the federal and state Endangered Species Acts, and the federal and state Wild and Scenic Rivers systems were created. In 1983, a significant court decision shook up long-established assumptions about water rights, water law, and the environment in California, though the decision that the Public Trust Doctrine applied to Mono Lake was not actually implemented until 1994. Other important changes in water law, meanwhile, came in 1992 with the Central Valley Project Improvement

Act, which returned 800,000 acre-feet of annual runoff to the environment. In 1993, the California Wetlands Conservation Policy was adopted, aiming for no net loss of wetlands in the state. Today, 28 percent of the state's water is dedicated by law to environmental uses in wetlands, in the San Francisco Bay and Sacramento–San Joaquin Delta, and in state and federally designated Wild and Scenic Rivers.

Of all of these developments, the decision that the Public Trust Doctrine applies to Mono Lake may have the broadest significance. The doctrine recognizes that government has a legal responsibility to protect resources with environmental and aesthetic values; such resources are held "in trust" for the public. The public trust protects the population's rights to use California's water resources for navigation, fisheries, commerce, environmental preservation, and recreation; as ecological units for scientific study; as open space; as environments that provide food and habitat for birds and marine life; and as environments favorably affecting the scenery and climate of the area. In the 1983 decision, the court also identified "changing public needs" for resource protection as requiring action by the government, adding, "Thus, the Public Trust is more than an affirmation of state power to use public property for public purposes. It is an affirmation of the duty of the state to protect the people's common heritage of streams, lakes, marshlands and tidelands, surrendering that right of protection only in rare cases when the abandonment of the right is consistent with the purposes of the Trust."

Application of the Public Trust Doctrine to Mono Lake rattled complacent water agencies in California. The city of Los Angeles had held legal water licenses authorizing its diversions from the Mono Basin for almost a half century. Despite that length of time, such water rights, the court held, must be reevaluated in the light of new information and changed societal values. Protection for the environment, however, was not absolute. Such values had to be *balanced* with beneficial domestic uses of diverted water. Los Angeles

Plate 103. Phalaropes at Mono Lake. Well over one million migratory and nesting birds visit the lake each year.

did not stop diverting water out of the Mono Basin, but it was required to reduce its take to levels that would also protect the Mono Lake ecosystem and its tributary streams.

Since 1941, four major streams that fed Mono Lake had been diverted into the Los Angeles Aqueduct. The complete dewatering of those streams also violated the state Fish and Game Code, and the court's decision also corrected that violation as well. Without the stream water to replace evaporation, Mono Lake lost half of its volume, and the salinity of its already harsh alkaline waters doubled. The unusually productive ecosystem, with its brine shrimp and Alkali Flies *(Ephydra hians)* that fed over a million migratory birds, was in danger of collapse. Island nesting habitat for the biggest breeding colony of California Gulls *(Larus californicus)* in the state had been connected to shore and invaded by coyotes as the lake dropped 45 vertical feet. (Pl. 103.)

The Mono Lake lawsuits were initiated by the National Audubon Society and the Mono Lake Committee, with Cal-Trout later suing separately over the dewatering of the streams. Under a plan ordered by the State Water Resources

Control Board in 1994, the lake will be managed at an elevation that still will be 27 feet below its prediversion level (a compromise that also recognizes beneficial uses of water diverted to Los Angeles). The recovery period, it was estimated in 1994, would last about 20 years.

"Save Mono Lake" messages on bumper stickers were replaced by "Long Live Mono Lake." Active stream and waterfowl habitat restoration measures were undertaken, recognizing that it could take centuries for the damaged streambeds to recover naturally and that lower lake levels will not ever restore original conditions for millions of ducks and geese that once used the lake.

## Restoration

Faced with the legal precedents established at Mono Lake, Los Angeles also settled lawsuits, in 1997, over the impacts its groundwater pumping had on the Owens Valley environment. That settlement agreement required Los Angeles to restore flows along 60 miles of the lower Owens River. Base flows of 40 cubic feet per second would increase to 200 cubic feet per second each spring, to recreate the flushing and sculpting actions of seasonal high runoff. The objective was a restored riparian corridor and warm-water fishery. When the Owens River water reached the north edge of Owens Lake, it would be pumped back into the Los Angeles Aqueduct. A little water (six to nine cubic feet per second) would pass the pumpback station and enter 1,100 acres of wetlands, where the river entered the lake. Controversy developed when Los Angeles failed to meet a deadline for the required environmental impact report and then proposed to triple the capacity of the pumpback station, so that less water could reach the delta.

As a result of separate legal requirements to address the air-polluting dust storms off the salty, dry lakebed, Los Angeles began spreading water with a system of delivery pipes and

Plate 104. Dust control bubblers putting water onto the Owens Lake bed to control dust storms that violate air quality standards.

"bubblers" in 2002 (pl. 104). Water is being applied to 22.5 square miles of the Owens Lake bed. Los Angeles must show compliance with clean air standards by 2006.

Legal precedents set by the Mono Lake decisions also governed restoration of salmon runs and natural river functions on the lower San Joaquin River. The Friant Water Users Authority and a consortium of 16 environmental groups, led by the Natural Resources Defense Council, agreed to work together toward a settlement plan to meet restoration goals without costing the water users any money or water. (Pl. 105.) The Vernalis Adaptive Management Plan has experimented with 31-day pulse flows in the spring, to benefit juvenile salmon migrating out to sea, and October "attraction" flows to help returning spawners locate their home waters. (Vernalis is the location where the San Joaquin River, with all of its tributary waters, enters the Delta.)

Efforts to restore 100,000 acres of San Francisco Bay's tidal marshlands were aided in 2002 when an agreement was announced to buy commercial salt ponds in the South Bay to restore waterfowl and wildlife habitat (pl. 106). In Humboldt

Plate 105. The San Joaquin River, one of California's largest river arteries, bone dry where it used to flow beneath Hwy. 152 near Los Banos. The river is dewatered below Friant Dam to serve agricultural irrigators.

Plate 106. The southern end of San Francisco Bay. Red and green mark commercial salt ponds. Boundary lines roughly delineate more than 16,000 acres acquired in 2002 to be restored as wetlands habitat.

Bay, in Northern California, water quality degradation had nearly destroyed natural values, but today 94 acres of wetlands are maintained by an innovative use of partially treated sewer effluent. Marsh vegetation thrives there as it cleans the discharged sewage water.

Restoration efforts have "captured the hearts and minds of

citizens throughout California," according to the SWRCB publication *Opportunity, Responsibility, Accountability: Nonpoint Source Pollution Control Program* (2001, 41). Understaffed state and local agencies increasingly rely on citizen volunteers to help with water quality monitoring. To document the effects of sediments entering Humboldt Bay from logging in that watershed, local volunteers, members of a group called "Salmon Forever," annually collect more than a thousand water quality samples from creeks and rivers entering the bay. The "Storm Water Detectives," a group of Lodi high school and middle school students given professional training, monitor insects and worms in the Mokelumne River. Their bioassessment data serve as one measure of river health. Other volunteers survey aquatic insects in the Truckee River downstream from Lake Tahoe and bacteria levels in the Yuba River. "DeltaKeeper" members identified very high levels of bacteria in popular swimming and water-skiing areas in the Delta, which led to federal listing of those waters as "impaired" (a Clean Water Act designation that triggers pollution management measures).

Such volunteers, according to the SWRCB, are "learning that streams are inseparable from their riparian corridors, and riparian corridors from their uplands—the watershed. All evolved together—each influenced by and influencing the other. They have come because they realize that whatever happens on the land eventually shows up in the stream at their feet, and they cannot heal the stream without healing the land" (2001, 41).

# CALFED

CALFED is an ambitious attempt by the state and federal governments to do something quixotic and perhaps impossible: end California's long history of water wars. No one (except, perhaps, certain lawyers) wants to face the costs and time required for complicated water litigation. The Bay-Delta Accord, which outlines basic principles and water quality standards to guide the program, was established in December 1994. Twenty-three state and federal agencies and many public and private groups participate in CALFED. They seek balanced solutions through consensus among "stakeholders." Those interested parties are generally categorized as "urban interests," "agriculture," and "environmental advocates."

CALFED intends to modify 188,000 acres of wetlands and streamside habitat, establish 385,000 "wildlife-friendly" agricultural acres, recharge underground aquifers, streamline water transfers, promote water use efficiency, clean contaminated agricultural runoff, and study the feasibility of building new reservoirs and of raising dams to increase storage. A major landmark in the 30-year effort comes in 2004, when "Decision and Review Points for Storage, Water Quality, and Water Use Efficiency Elements" will be published. CALFED is addressing many of California's statewide water challenges. It has funded projects on more than 70 percent of California's landscape, across 40,000 square miles of watershed lands. Many restoration efforts have focused on the Sacramento–San Joaquin watershed, including fish passage improvements along 182 river-miles and 64 new fish screens at diversion points (pl. 107). The two-year budget begun in July 2001 relied upon $508 million from the state, $81 million in federal funds, and $263 million from other sources (primarily water agencies).

Although serving statewide water objectives, the effort focuses on the Bay-Delta and the river systems in its watershed, because drinking water for 22 million Californians passes through the Delta bottleneck, along with water for much of the state's agricultural land. The dual role of the estuary as a water project dispersal point and as critical habitat for many endangered and threatened species had been straining the system. Water users were motivated to correct environmental conditions as a way to improve both the quality of the water

Plate 107. Fish screen improvement work on the intake of an irrigation district diversion from the lower Sacramento River. This project was partially funded by CALFED.

coming to them from the Delta and its reliability, so that pumping from the Delta might not so often be curtailed.

Chris Robinson, a rancher along the Merced River (where CALFED funding was used to restore salmon spawning habitat), explained the reasoning in CALFED's 2001 annual report: "You redesign the river, you restore it to a more natural functioning, and *hopefully you need less water to make the system work the way it's supposed to—everybody wins*" (2002, 19; italics added).

Whether leaving less water in the river means that "everybody wins" is the multibillion-dollar question. The answer will determine whether all the interests now willing to fund these programs and work with CALFED continue their participation. The three stakeholder categories may not accurately reflect the real range of values. "Agricultural interests" include farmers and related agribusinesses, but also many of California's "farm" corporations that, history shows, are as interested in real estate development as in long-term agriculture. "Environmental organizations" have memberships that are overwhelmingly urban, yet their goals are generally very different from those of the stakeholders labeled "urban inter-

Plate 108. Cranes, at dawn, in the seasonally flooded wetlands of the Cosumnes River Preserve.

ests." That group includes public-service water providers, but also interests that focus most on overcoming water limits that would curtail growth and development. Establishing consensus allowed the process to begin, but it may ultimately be impossible for CALFED to do everything for everyone. There may be little room for compromise when a species is endangered; extinction is an absolute condition. Looming over the entire effort is the fact that political and financial power resides overwhelmingly with some of the urban interests, held in "balance" solely by environmental protection laws and the long-established water rights of many farmers. Environmental and agricultural stakeholders face the insatiable, seemingly never-ending thirst of urban interests that, for the most part, are unwilling to realistically consider adjusting their own water needs toward long-term stability.

Meanwhile, one of CALFED's goals has been to promote set-back levees to enable rivers to make wider use of floodplains, breaking the pattern of straitjacketing rivers in narrow channels between armored bank levees. The benefits will be improved water quality, as vegetation filters pollution from reaching waterways, and more wildlife habitat, shade, and food for fish. The objective is complicated because so much building has occurred on floodplains, but at the Cosumnes River Preserve, on a watershed that has no dams to hold back flood-water, straitjacket levees have been breached. The first breach came in 1985 and was accidental. After that flood event deposited sediments, cottonwoods and willows sprouted and created an "accidental" forest that became a mosaic of 40-foot-high trees and willow thickets as the years passed. In 1995, another levee gap was cut on purpose. That created an "intentional" forest. Both forests keep erosion back from the Cosumnes River, filter pollutants, provide habitat, and reduce flood risks to neighboring areas. This was a cooperative project of the Nature Conservancy, the U.S. Bureau of Land Management, the Department of Fish and Game, Ducks Unlimited, Sacramento County, and the Department of Water Resources. (Pl. 108.)

CALFED has been studying five surface storage projects, including new off-stream reservoirs and the enlargement of some existing dams. Dams are controversial. Senator Dianne Feinstein, in an opinion piece in the *San Francisco Chronicle* (August 1, 2001) advocating federal funding of CALFED, wrote: "There are those who would challenge any effort to increase the amount of water stored during wet years for use during dry years as potentially damaging to the ecosystem. And there are those who want iron-clad assurance a full allocation of water will be available for agriculture and urban use no matter what damage this could cause to the environment. We can provide more off-stream water storage and restore the endangered ecosystem. It should not be one or the other."

# The Debate over Dams

Some of the problems that dams create for salmon are being addressed by CALFED through modifications to existing structures and changes in the way dams are operated (pl. 109). At Shasta Dam, a new temperature control device allows operators to pull water from different depths, rather than solely off the warm surface of the reservoir. Salmon require cold water, around 56 degrees F, during critical times when eggs hatch and fry emerge. To ensure that cold water can be released from April through September, more storage must be held in Shasta Reservoir.

Plate 109. Red Bluff Dam with the gates up to allow salmon to pass.

Between 1995 and 2010, 51 hydropower licenses affecting 212 dams have come or will come up for their first renewal. Hydropower licenses were issued by the Federal Energy Regulatory Commission (FERC) for periods of 30 to 50 years. Though hydropower is a clean form of energy production, diversions through power plants impact streams. Some have diverted 90 percent of the natural flow in rivers. Relicensing presents an opportunity to adjust operating requirements to ecologically based in-stream flow needs. The trade-off will be lost power generation capacity. The process requires studies on fish, water temperatures, passage of sediments and gravels, and historic flow patterns. It will establish minimum in-stream flows that mimic nature and are supported by science. CalTrout has called the FERC relicensing process "the single greatest opportunity to restore coldwater fisheries in California over the next decade."

# Build More Behemoths?

The era of major dam building has ended; all the suitable sites for large dams in river canyons in California have been developed. The last major dam built in California was the New Melones Dam on the Stanislaus River, completed in 1979. One project, the Auburn Dam, was halted 25 years ago but seems to have become the "never-ending story" in water politics. The dam was originally proposed to store water, generate electricity, and create a recreational reservoir on the north and middle forks of the American River. The first design, for a 700-foot-tall thin-arch dam, was abandoned because of earthquake risks. Later plans called for a smaller, redesigned dam solely to reduce the risk of floods reaching Sacramento. It would have cost over $1 billion. Friends of the American River opposed that proposal, pointing to more than 500,000 recreational users of the river canyon and its white-water rafting stretches every year. They also claimed there was a greater likelihood of a reservoir-induced quake than of the 500-year flood the dam was supposed to prevent.

The debates generated more of the hyperbole that has characterized California's long history of water development. On December 31, 2001, the *Sacramento Bee* quoted a former Nevada County supervisor as saying, "This state is not going to survive unless we impound more water. We need Auburn dam."

Despite such dire warnings, the Bureau of Reclamation, in fall 2002, did something historically rare for that agency: it closed the tunnel that diverted water from its dam construction site, 35 years after initial construction began in 1967, and let the river run again through its historic channel. Some saw this decision as a signal of a major change of values and attitudes about rivers in California. Whether the Auburn Dam is truly dead remains to be seen.

New storage possibilities upstream from Friant Dam in the San Joaquin River watershed are being considered, including possible construction of Temperance Flat Reservoir on the site that some people preferred when Friant Dam was first considered. The new storage water might figure into the restoration efforts on the lower San Joaquin, along with management of agricultural water downstream. But nonstructural options also exist for increasing water supply from the Friant system, including enlarged outlets or spillway gates. Enlargement of Friant Dam itself and construction of an off-stream dam to create Fine Gold Creek Reservoir are other options the Bureau of Reclamation is considering. Its "Upper San Joaquin River Basin Storage Investigation" will not reach a decision point until 2006.

## Off-Stream Dams?

With all of the best dam sites along rivers long since developed, off-stream storage reservoirs, filled by pumping water from other sites into dry canyons, are most often promoted now to increase water supplies. Off-stream dams are intended to increase management flexibility, making water available at different times and places than nature provides it. The MWD recently completed a huge off-stream reservoir south of the San Bernardino Mountains, near Hemet, with a 12-mile tunnel through the mountains to deliver water to the coastal plain. The Diamond Valley Reservoir can hold a six-month supply for the MWD's customers, should earthquake, terrorism, or drought interrupt flow along the aqueducts. (Pl. 110.)

CALFED is considering a dam near the town of Sites, in Colusa County, to store 1.9 million acre-feet. It would be filled from the Sacramento River during wet seasons for use during dry periods. Construction costs could be as much as $1.6 billion, so the water would cost around $450 per acre-foot, at the expensive end of the range of prices paid in Southern California. The dam is intended to provide flexibility in water management, rather than affordable water, with environmental benefits possible for Delta water quality and fisheries protec-

Plate 110. MWD's new Diamond Valley Reservoir, near Hemet. This reservoir was filled in 2002 with water from the north (the SWP) and from the east (the Colorado River).

tion flows. One concern about the project is that reducing high runoff in the Sacramento River may further reduce natural cleansing and gravel movements.

Los Vaqueros Reservoir is an existing off-stream reservoir in Contra Costa County, east of San Francisco Bay, with 100,000 acre-feet of storage that CALFED may expand to 500,000. Decisions about the Sites and Los Vaqueros projects are to be made by the end of 2004.

# Raise Existing Dams?

The "Upper San Joaquin River Basin Storage Investigation" includes, as one possibility, raising Friant Dam to store an additional 700,000 acre-feet. Similarly, the Bureau of Reclamation has conducted an "Appraisal Assessment" on possibilities for enlarging Shasta Dam. Three enlargement options were evaluated: raising the crest of Shasta Dam by 6.5, 102.5, or 202.5 feet. The bureau concluded that the 6.5-foot raise was the most viable project for further analysis. The enlarged reservoir would store an additional 290,000 acre-feet, cost $122 million, take four years to construct, and flood 780 acres along several miles of the upper Sacramento, the McCloud, and the Pit Rivers. Both the upper Sacramento and the McCloud are pristine river habitat, identified as eligible for federal Wild and Scenic River status. The McCloud lost 15 of its 35 miles when the original Shasta Reservoir was created. Sacred sites and burial grounds of the Winnemem Wintu Indians lie beneath the reservoir. Raising the dam would flood another mile of the McCloud, inundating most of the remaining sacred sites along the river. The decision point for Shasta enlargement will come in 2004.

The city of Sacramento could achieve 213-year flood protection along the American River if Folsom Dam were raised seven feet, according to an Army Corps of Engineers report in 2001. Sacramento has already substantially increased its degree of flood protection without raising the dam. After 1986 storms came close to overwhelming levees, 19 miles of the American River levee system were improved, increasing flood protection to a 100-year level. Widening the release outlets at

Plate 111. Sacramento River, confined between levees to protect homes and farms from floods.

Plate 112. Secretary of the Interior Bruce Babbitt using a sledgehammer to begin the historic dismantling of a small dam on Butte Creek in the Sacramento Valley in 1998.

Folsom Dam is a separate project to give the area 140-year protection. That is expected to eliminate a current requirement that most properties obtain flood insurance. (Pl. 111.)

## Raze Existing Dams?

Dams are not forever. Each has a life expectancy; sediments will fill them all, in time. Given the impacts dams have had on some species in California, it is important to keep in mind that "extinction is forever, dams are not."

Between 1920 and 1956, 22 dams were removed along 100 river-miles in the watershed of the Klamath River, a North Coast river that carries heavy sediment loads. In 1969, the city of Eureka blew up Sweasey Dam on the Mad River, which had completely filled with silt.

There are other reasons to remove a dam. Small irrigation diversion dams were removed from Butte Creek, in the Sacramento Valley, to restore 25 miles of unimpeded flow for migrating salmon. Farmers still received their irrigation water, through redesigned systems, but the creek itself flowed free. Thousands of fish began using the channel during the next migratory seasons. Secretary of the Interior Bruce Babbitt helped celebrate the 1998 dam removal (pl. 112). Babbitt told reporters, "We're not taking aim at all dams, but we should strike a balance between the needs of the river and the demands of river users…. In all probability the process will continue on a dam-by-dam basis, with states and community stakeholders making most decisions. But there can be no doubt that we have a long way to go toward a better balance" (Friends of the River 1999, 2).

Plate 113. "Restore Hetch Hetchy" bumper sticker.

CALFED has adopted dam removal as one of the tools it may use for restoring habitat and the ecological functioning of rivers. Whenever a dam is considered for demolition, cleanup and handling of the sediment trapped behind it must be addressed. The costs of removal have to be balanced with the costs of attempted repairs or improvements to dams nearing the end of their useful lives. For most very large dams, renovation may be very difficult.

In 2000, 87 years after Congress authorized construction of a dam in Hetch Hetchy Valley, the head of the Restore Hetch Hetchy organization authored "The Hetchysburg Address," which opened, "Four score and seven years ago, our fathers brought forth upon this continent a new dam and reservoir, conceived in the Bay Area, and dedicated to the proposition that all national parks are not created equal. Now we are engaged in a great debate—testing whether that dam and reservoir, or any things so conceived and so dedicated—should any longer endure." (Pl. 113.)

Restore Hetch Hetchy? What would San Francisco and the other Bay Area cities using Tuolumne River water do for a supply, if O'Shaughnessy Dam were taken down? As shocking as the idea seemed, in 1988 Secretary of the Interior Donald Hodel suggested that the restoration of Hetch Hetchy might be feasible *without* reducing the city's water supply. The con-

Plate 114. New Don Pedro Reservoir, which could replace Hetch Hetchy Reservoir storage.

cept was not to take the SFPUC's water away, but to replumb the Tuolumne River water delivery system. A capital improvement program already includes plans to enlarge Calaveras Reservoir, in Alameda County, to nearly twice the capacity of Hetch Hetchy Reservoir. Other storage options might involve changes in operation of New Don Pedro Reservoir, downstream from Hetch Hetchy (pl. 114), to pass along more water to Calaveras, or possibly to coordinate with the proposed expansion of Los Vaqueros Reservoir in Contra Costa County. Even new plumbing to send Tuolumne water over to take advantage of storage space in New Melones Reservoir on the Stanislaus River has been suggested. To deliver additional water could require a fourth pipeline across the Central Valley. The goal of the Restore Hetch Hetchy organization is to have dam removal under way by 2013, the 100th anniversary of the Raker Act.

Restoration of the scenic valley in Yosemite National Park would require removal of the sediments trapped by the dam. The report prepared for Interior Secretary Hodel concluded that "within two years extensive areas on the floor of Hetch Hetchy Valley would be covered with grasses, sedges, rushes, and other herbaceous plants that would be highly visible." It would take longer for trees and shrubs to grow, and it might take decades for the "bathtub ring" to disappear along the canyon walls. Full restoration could take a century, but it could be accelerated by active restoration measures. The Hodel report noted that there would be less electrical output from hydroelectric plants in the SFPUC system. The first priority of the Hetch Hetchy system has been water supply; in droughts, water has been held back though it meant cuts in electricity generation.

San Francisco's multibillion-dollar effort to renovate its more than 80-year-old infrastructure presents an opportunity to think the unthinkable. Restoration of Hetch Hetchy Valley to Yosemite National Park would be a gift to the nation and to the world, an amazing gift to our children and grandchildren. John Muir would be enormously pleased.

# Storage in the Bank

Because we have overdrafted and depleted groundwater basins, an opportunity exists for increased water storage in those aquifers. Groundwater basins can provide "water in the bank" savings accounts to help during dry climate cycles. "Conjunctive use" is the term water agencies have adopted to describe the deliberate coordination of surface water with groundwater supplies. Groundwater storage has several advantages over reservoirs. It produces none of the evaporation loss, is ordinarily less vulnerable to pollution, and reduces the impacts of dams and canals on habitat and natural water-courses. Like off-stream reservoirs, water banking does not create more water but adds to the developed supply, stretching its availability and flexibility. Banking can only add "new" water to the state's supply budget if the water is captured during flood events that would otherwise send it out to the ocean, or the groundwater basin is filled using recycled wastewater that would otherwise be sent out to sea.

The Kern Water Bank in the southern San Joaquin Valley near Bakersfield may be the state's most successful facility of this type. In the 1980s, the SWP purchased 19,000 acres along the Kern River, near Bakersfield. The state never operated a "bank" there but gave the land to the Kern County Water Agency in 1994 (in exchange for forgiveness of payments on 45,000 acre-feet of contracted water). The 30 square miles of valley floor are on an alluvial fan that is ideal for percolating water into the ground; it can absorb over a half foot each day. Theoretically, the bank will be able to store one million acre-feet and extract about 240,000 acre-feet in a year. By 2002, the bank held about 870,000 acre-feet of SWP or CVP water not previously needed by contractors. Recovery was handled by 80 wells. To make these systems valuable beyond a local area's needs, interconnections between aqueducts and canals are necessary. The Kern Water Bank can use the Cross Valley Canal and its own canal to send water westward to the California Aqueduct or eastward toward the Friant-Kern Canal (pl. 115). Another benefit of the program has been reestablishment of intermittent wetlands habitat in that part of the San Joaquin Valley, which had been converted to farmland. Some waterfowl species are appearing there that had not been seen in the area for over 70 years. Native upland habitat is also being reestablished on one-third of the bank's lands.

The MWD is a client of the Kern Water Bank and of the SemiTropic Water Bank, also in the southern San Joaquin Valley. With another conjunctive-use project in Ventura County,

Plate 115. Water recovered from storage beneath the ground at the Kern Water Bank, to be sent to the California Aqueduct for customers farther south.

the MWD had 910,000 acre-feet in groundwater storage accounts in 2002. Another, more controversial MWD groundwater-banking project was proposed in the Mojave Desert in eastern San Bernardino County. Using private land owned by the Cadiz Corporation, the MWD would have paid to store underground up to one million acre-feet from the Colorado River, but also planned to pump "native" water from that groundwater basin. This was one of the ways the MWD hoped to implement the federally mandated 4.4 Plan, as California tried to live within its allocation from the Colorado River. Concerns developed because dry-year extraction of up to 150,000 acre-feet from the Cadiz Basin might have exceeded the natural recharge capacity and damaged the desert environment. A dispute developed when USGS scientists estimated that the pumping rate proposed might be 25 times the rate of replacement by precipitation. The proponents pledged to monitor the situation with wells, but skeptics worried that once the pumps, canals, and wells were in place, thirsty desert creatures in a distant valley would not have as much pull as millions of thirsty Southern Californians. The situation had disturbing parallels to Los Angeles's export of Owens Valley surface water and groundwater. In October 2002, the MWD board voted to cancel this project.

The Orange County Water District's Groundwater Replenishment System puts more than 100 million gallons per day of wastewater treated to better than drinking-water standards into the coastal groundwater basin. Recharging with freshwater holds back salty seawater that otherwise moves inland underground and contaminates city wells.

All this attention to groundwater management has renewed interest in, and opposition to, laws that might provide statewide groundwater management for the first time. Farmers and irrigation districts, in particular, seemed adamantly opposed, arguing that local conditions varied so much that local control was the only proper response. A Groundwater Management Act passed in 1992 allows local water agencies to voluntarily develop groundwater management plans and coordinate surface and groundwater supplies. Concerns about sales of groundwater to other regions led to a court case, settled in 1994, that affirmed that county governments share power with the state and special districts to regulate such transfers. To clarify its authority over groundwater, the State Water Resources Control Board asked Joseph Sax of the UC Berkeley Law School to evaluate the relevant laws.

The SWRCB was given permitting authority only over surface and "subterranean stream water." The question was what lawmakers envisioned by the latter category, as opposed to a third legal category, "percolating groundwater." Sax wrote, "The above categories do not accord with scientific understanding of the occurrence and distribution of water on and in the earth. To hydrogeologists, water is a continuum." To that restatement of basic water cycle facts, he added, "From a technical perspective, the distinction between percolating groundwater and subterranean streams is meaningless, or nearly so." Despite ambiguous wording, Sax concluded, the legislature had intended the state to intervene whenever it could be shown that human activities had an impact on groundwater. Despite Sax's conclusions, the SWRCB, in May 2002, declined to assert more authority over California's groundwater, in the face of major counterpressure from agricultural and urban interests.

## Transfers: Water as a Commodity

Underground water banking could be confused with something quite different, the California Drought Water Bank, which was an emergency drought measure to coordinate the sale of surface water to needy buyers. In 1991, in the fourth year of an extended drought, Governor Pete Wilson issued an executive order creating the Drought Water Bank. The bank purchased surface water from willing sellers and sold it to buyers experiencing critical shortages. The water was made available by fallowing farmland or substituting groundwater for the marketed surface water. The bank operated in 1991, 1992, and 1994. It was not a permanent solution to the long-term reality of droughts, and definitely not something that communities or agencies experiencing shortages could count on when planning development.

Historically, Californians have not paid for water itself. Paying a water bill feels like buying water, but the bill actually covers only the costs of storage, treatment, and delivery to the tap. Water in California cannot be "bought" because all of it is owned by the state. There have long been legal obstacles to moving water from agriculture to urban users. The state legislature and the federal CVPIA have now cleared these away, so that water can be marketed as a commodity. State Water Code provisions still require that there be no adverse effects on other water rights holders and no unreasonable effects on fish and wildlife resources.

Given that water is essential for life, it is amazing how little philosophical debate preceded this move into the market. The philosophy that the free market can best manage anything is being given another test, somewhat like the test Californians were subjected to regarding electricity deregulation. Several philosophical questions deserved more attention than they received before the obstacles were removed:

If water is to be sold only to those who will meet a seller's price, where does that leave the poor? And how will the environment compete?

How can we balance the vital life-giving functions of water in the California landscape against the use of water simply for convenience or comfort?

How much care will be taken to assure that real water is being marketed, rather than "paper water," which may be based on water rights that cannot be satisfied?

Do we want to encourage "water ranching" by land speculators who acquire real estate just to sell water taken away from it?

Because water is vital for life, governments must manage the resource for the common good. Regulation is needed to protect the public trust. In 1977, the United Nations proclaimed, "All people…have the right to have access to drinking water in quantities and of a quality equal to their basic needs." In July 2001, at a Water for People and Nature meeting in Vancouver, delegates from 35 countries proposed an international treaty to declare "that the global fresh water supply is a shared legacy, a public trust, and a fundamental human right" that should not be "sold by an institution, government, individual, or corporation for profit." (Barlow and Clarke 2002, xvii, xviii.)

California has headed in another direction. "In California," a saying goes, "water flows uphill toward money." Norris Hundley Jr.'s pessimistic conclusion (in *The Great Thirst,* 2001, 519) was, "With water, like land, now subject to a market system and allowed to go blindly to the highest and most powerful bidders—invariably metropolitan areas and developers—the future holds little promise of being fundamentally different from the past." Although CALFED has created an environmental water fund to attempt to enter the market to secure water for environmental needs, many are leery about such a fund's ability to realistically compete against urban demands.

In 2001, water transfers moved 637,000 acre-feet, enough for the annual needs of five million people. That year the MWD began negotiating an agreement to pay Palo Verde Valley farmers (along the Colorado River near Blythe) to stop growing food on about 30 percent of their fields, releasing up to 110,000 acre-feet of water each year to the MWD. Over the 35 years of the plan, the district could spend up to $337 million to secure 3.6 million acre-feet of water. The deal would not provide any "new" water for the MWD but would replace some of the "surplus" Colorado River water that California must stop using. The MWD had to negotiate individual deals with farmers who held the water rights. The MWD would make one-time payments of $3,170 for each acre set aside. It also would make annual payments that could total more than growers receive from their crops in some years. Agriculture was the primary economy in the valley, where 37,000 people resided. The MWD said that the impact on the local farm economy would be minimal, because only the least productive land would be set aside. Farmers were not so certain but have showed interest in the deal, in part because they perceived the political clout of urban areas as so great that their water might be taken away forcibly, if the societal decision was that urban needs were the "highest use."

Farmers had learned a lesson about urban clout when they resisted pressure to transfer water to San Diego. When the December 31, 2002, deadline arrived without an agreement on the 4.4 Plan, meant to gradually wean California from its overuse of Colorado River water, the Department of the Interior announced immediate cuts for the MWD (instead of the

15-year gradual cutback that a plan would have triggered). The department also, however, declared that the Imperial Irrigation District would lose over 200,000 acre-feet of its historic water allotments to the MWD. The IID had previously balked at a plan to annually sell up to 200,000 acre-feet to the San Diego County Water Authority. The IID board had objected to the land fallowing that this sale would have required. Despite proposed payments to farmers, cuts in acreage would have echoed through the valley's economy and population. The IID board also wanted water interests pushing the transfer to share some of the district's liability for the damages that would result to the Salton Sea environment when fallowing reduced the amount of water reaching the sea.

The competing pressures of agriculture, urban growth, and the environment had never been so clear. One plan for Salton Sea "restoration" bowed to the enormous political and financial clout of urban interests. The Pacific Institute suggested that lesser amounts of water flowing to the sea be concentrated into a smaller area, confined by dikes, where salinities suitable for fish and waterfowl could be maintained. The main portion of the sea would become hypersaline, something akin to Mono Lake.

Far to the north, a proposal to capture freshwater from the mouths of the Albion and Gualala Rivers could have generated fleets of tugboats traveling from the Mendocino coast to San Diego. The boats would tow water bags the size of three football fields—100 feet wide, 800 feet long, and 25 feet deep—each holding 16 acre-feet. The plan faced major opposition from local residents, along with reviews by the local county, the California Coastal Commission, and the SWRCB. Interest in San Diego was contingent on the price being realistically close to the $444 per acre-foot charged by the MWD. The entrepreneur abandoned the initial proposal but shifted his efforts toward buying, bagging, and towing water purchased from the Humboldt Bay Municipal Water District for sale to either San Diego or Monterey. In a news story about the earlier scheme, a North Coast resident was quoted (in the *Santa Rosa Press Democrat,* March 17, 2002): "When people in San Diego empty their swimming pools and close down the golf courses, then maybe I'll take some of this seriously." Wiser use of existing supplies would, in fact, diminish the motivation behind such controversial water sales.

## Short-Cutting the Cycle

An alternative to the historic practice of pumping treated wastewater from coastal cities out to sea is reusing it. Recycled water (also called "reclaimed" water) is a drought-proof source of supply, because it is already "in hand" and affected very little by weather cycles. In addition, it does not have to be imported from hundreds of miles away. Recycling is one of the many little "water wheels," both natural and man-made, that are shortcuts within the great planetary water cycle.

Traditional wastewater treatments remove solids and add disinfectants such as chlorine. Recycling relies upon additional methods to produce "designer water." Reverse osmosis forces water through very fine pores of microfilter membranes. Such filtration, along with ultraviolet light treatments, can remove even medical wastes, antibiotics, birth control drugs, and antidepressant drugs dissolved in wastewater. Typical drinking water carries fine particles in the 500 parts per million range. Reverse osmosis takes that down to just 50 parts per million. Orange County has new treatment plants that are aiming at three parts per *billion.*

State law limits the uses of recycled water to concrete plants, snowmaking, freeway landscaping, commercial laundries, fountains, golf courses, schoolyard lawns, and crop irrigation. It can also be used to recharge groundwater aquifers (though that use is closely controlled and monitored). In 1991, the Irvine Ranch Water District (IRWD) became the first water district in the nation with health department ap-

Plate 116. A City of Irvine park. The city uses recycled water in fountains and for landscape irrigation in its parks.

proval for *interior* use of reclaimed water. High-rise offices ran reclaimed water through separate toilet-flushing systems identified by purple pipes. Drinking water used within the specially plumbed buildings dropped by as much as 75 percent, because it was no longer being flushed down toilets. Overall, about 20 percent of the water in Irvine's system was reclaimed, conserving more than 19,000 acre-feet a year. "Water is too valuable to be used just once," according to the IRWD. (Pl. 116.)

Golf courses, parks, and freeway landscapes use the most reclaimed water. Los Angeles has a goal of reusing 40 percent of its wastewater by 2010. The MWD recycled 190,000 acre-feet in 2001. ExxonMobil's refinery in Torrance saves 4,250 gallons every minute by using reclaimed water as a coolant. Marin County has 25 miles of underground pipes to deliver treated wastewater to car washes and to toilets in the county jail and in a convalescent home. The return is an average savings of one million gallons a day. Sonoma County vineyards irrigated with reclaimed water use up to 15,000 acre-feet of recycled water every year. An additional 2,000 acre-feet go to the Sonoma County Water Agency for landscape irrigation.

Despite the savings and the benefits to the environment of not importing water from distant watersheds, concerns were expressed when Los Angeles planned the East Valley Water Reclamation Project. These new recycling plants would have recharged San Gabriel Valley groundwater basins (to partly make up for water no longer diverted from Mono Lake streams). The Miller Brewing Company was opposed, worried that its products could be suspect because they used the groundwater. It later dropped its opposition, but when the San Fernando Valley considered seceding from the city (for unrelated reasons), the mayor of Los Angeles was wary of political fallout and ordered the Department of Water and Power (DWP) not to start the project. Citizens in the Livermore and Amador Valleys voted down a groundwater recharge program. In 1999, San Diego voters rejected a plan to put treated water into a local reservoir. Opponents branded the practice "from toilet to tap."

Of course, *all* of Earth's water is recycled. "Wastewater" is just a temporary status until natural processes of the water

Plate 117. Urban dwellers reconnecting with the fascinations of water at the public fountain at Cesar Chavez Plaza in San Jose. Recycling reduces the inevitable losses to evaporation.

cycle turn it back into "beverage." The 22 million Californians who drink water taken from the Delta should realize that their supply includes a portion that has passed through the waste systems of over a half dozen cities upstream along the Sacramento River. Much of Orange County's water from regional sources has already been used in San Bernardino and Riverside Counties, farther up the Santa Ana River watershed.

Although the purity of water from treatment plants is something that should concern people and be insisted upon, recycling efforts generate tremendous benefits. Across California, we now reuse more than 400,000 acre-feet annually, enough for 800,000 homes or about 3.2 million people. The 1998 California Water Plan estimated that recycling could potentially total 1.4 million acre-feet by 2020, or about two percent of the state's water supply. If those percentages increase, safely, we will all benefit. (Pl. 117.)

# Squeezing the Sponge

Another way to generate "new" supplies of water is simply to make wiser use of water and stretch the existing supply. Conservation measures thoroughly "squeeze the sponge." They proved their practicality during the drought of 1987 to 1992, but as soon as droughts end, daily habits tend to revert to extravagance. In conserving, as in recycling, it makes sense to focus less on the extra effort and more on the positive benefits of frugal behaviors and attitudes.

The assumption used for many years that one acre-foot served the annual needs of five people was actually extravagant. In Los Angeles, where DWP customers have been given modern low-flush toilets for free, an acre-foot today serves eight people. DWP has given away over a million toilets that only use 1.6 gallons per flush. (Pl. 118.) Old toilets use 3.5 to seven gallons every time they are flushed. Because toilets account for 40 percent of the water used in households, this

Plate 118. Publicity for free low-flush toilets for Los Angeles Department of Water and Power customers.

Plate 119. A hose running while a car is washed. A spray nozzle can stop this waste of water.

retrofitting program allowed the Los Angeles population to grow by 32 percent after 1970, without increasing the amount of water the city consumed. National law now requires toilets that are sold or installed to use no more than 1.6 gallons per flush. If you are still using an old toilet, you should consider a replacement. Sticking with an older model, even one that still works just fine, is actually the greater waste.

Modern washing machines have also been redesigned to improve water and energy efficiency. Front-loading machines do not fully immerse clothes, instead rotating them through a pool of water. They require 25 to 35 percent less water than standard washers, or 16 gallons less per load.

It is strange that we keep large water heaters full of hot water 24 hours a day. On-demand hot water systems end the wasteful running of cold water down the drain while waiting for it to get hot. They can save 30 gallons per day.

Behaviors and habits can be the most important conservation methods. Running faucets can consume two to five gallons every minute! It makes no sense to leave water running while you brush teeth or shave; turn it off after wetting the brush or rinsing the razor, and you can save three or more gallons each time. Running water down the drain while waiting for it to get colder is a thoughtless waste of about two gallons of water. If you are prone to that mistake, try keeping a cold pitcher in the refrigerator. If you are looking for hot water, run the cold stuff into a pitcher while waiting for it to get hot and use that to water houseplants or for later drinking. And never thaw frozen food under *running* water; what a waste! There are better ways to thaw food, particularly now that microwaves are common appliances.

Water and brooms should not be confused. Five minutes of hosing the sidewalk or driveway can waste 25 gallons of water. Put a shut-off nozzle on the hose for washing the car and turn it off until running water is required. (Pl. 119.) Leaving the hose running for 20 minutes while washing a car can use 100 to 200 gallons of water! And if you take your car to a commercial car wash, ask if they recycle their water. Many do; all should.

If you wash dishes in the sink by hand, fill the basin, rather than leaving the water running, and save 25 gallons. Do not start dishwashers until they are fully loaded. Study that dial on the washer and take advantage of the short-cycle option; you can save three to four gallons per wash. If you use the toilet as a wastebasket or ashtray, consider the better alternatives, but more critically, avoid flushing *that* stuff. Let it sit until there is a *real* need to flush.

Leaky faucets are insidious. They are a pain to repair, but day in and day out, they deliver water straight from the tap to the sewer, without any beneficial use along the way. Sixty drips per minute can waste 190 gallons per month, more than six gallons each day. A "silent leak" in the toilet can keep 30 to 50 gallons a day running through the pipes and down the drain.

Think about how many showers are taken in your household. Low-flow showerheads may save 10 gallons of water every time they are used. If someone in your family loves long, slow showers, ask him or her to put a bucket in the shower someday to trap just a portion of the water, then use the results to start a discussion about how much water goes down the drain.

In warm parts of California where swimming pools are popular, 100 gallons of heated water may evaporate each day from a single pool, totaling about 3,000 gallons per month. Use a pool cover, not just to help reduce heating costs, but to minimize evaporation when the pool is not being used.

Landscaping appropriate to a dry climate can save fantastic amounts of water. Lawns should be watered in the evening or the morning, so less evaporates immediately and the water has a chance to soak into the root zone. A 1,000-square-foot lawn can require 2,100 to 3,600 gallons each month. Consider a smaller lawn and, depending on your local climate and the season, water every other or every third day. Give yourself or your gardener a break from frequent lawn mowing, and set the mower to cut higher; grass grown two to three inches high blankets the soil and reduces evaporation. At the agency level, the Municipal Water District of Orange County began giving away thousands of home-sprinkler systems controlled by a sophisticated central system that monitors local weather and automatically sends on-off instructions via pagers. (Pl. 120.)

The California Urban Water Conservation Council has identified Best Management Practices (BMPs) and secured a commitment from about 100 urban water suppliers to institute BMPs that provide the conservation benefits of low-flow showerheads, low-flush toilets, leak detection programs, metering, tiered pricing, and public information campaigns. BMP implementation has been slow but could reduce demand by 1.5 million acre-feet by 2020, according to the 1998 California Water Plan. Amazingly, some major cities in California, including Sacramento and Fresno, have not yet even installed water meters, the most basic pay-for-what-you-use incentives.

Plate 120. Sprinkling the road, the sidewalk, the driveway, and, incidentally, the lawn. A simple adjustment would save many gallons of water.

# Clean Water

We all can help minimize the pollution generated by such a large population by picking up after our pets and disposing of droppings either in the toilet or in trash that goes to a landfill. We should keep outside trash cans covered, keep leaf piles away from gutters and drains, minimize or stop using pesticides on lawns and gardens, never hose down sidewalks or driveways, and support community projects to ultimately divert drain water into treatment facilities or into the ground, the route it once naturally followed.

In 2002, the Los Angeles RWQCB adopted new requirements for water quality in Santa Monica Bay. It was finally complying with a 1979 deadline set in the federal Clean Water Act, in response to legal pressure from organizations such as

Santa Monica BayKeeper, the NRDC, and Heal the Bay. The requirements allow another three years for meeting state bacterial standards at beaches in the summer, and six years to achieve winter dry weather standards equivalent to natural conditions (as if no human sources of bacteria were present). They apply to all beaches in Ventura and Los Angeles Counties.

Achieving cleanup of storm runoff will be a much tougher accomplishment. The Irvine Ranch Water District has plans to build dozens of artificial wetlands throughout central Orange County to clean up contaminated water. The success of such efforts was demonstrated in Humboldt Bay, far to the north. Wetlands will work as well as traditional drainage and treatment facilities and cost less in the long run. They also should provide side benefits as wildlife habitat and bird-watching spots for humans.

The Chino Basin dairy water pollution issues have been addressed by trucking manure out of the basin, but the Inland Empire Utilities Agency has also committed to a 12 million gallons per day desalination facility for removing the nitrates in groundwater saturated by cow wastes. Manure actually helps power the desalination plant to start an elegant cleanup and recycling chain: methane gas is harvested from composting cow manure and used to generate electricity, which runs the desalter, which augments the local water supply.

## Lemonade from Lemons

Can desalination plants augment the entire state's water supply by tapping into the ocean water off the California coast? In every discussion about water limits, that idea is raised. "Water, water everywhere, and not a drop to drink." Can we turn it into "drink"?

Most desalination plants in California are similar to the Inland Empire Utilities Agency's: they are inland and do not process seawater. Instead, they treat brackish groundwater with high levels of dissolved solids from sewer effluent or other contaminants, or seawater intrusion. These systems require less expensive filter membranes than do plants that treat seawater.

Avalon, on Catalina Island, was the first California town to desalinate seawater. The city of Santa Barbara built a desalination facility in 1992 capable of producing 7,500 acre-feet per year. The city decided to invest in the plant at the end of a long drought, but ran it for only three months. It has been shut down ever since, because cheaper water became readily available when the drought ended. Some of the equipment was subsequently sold, leaving a current capacity of 3,125 acre-feet.

Oceanside, dependent on the MWD for water, built a desalting plant in 1994, prompted by the drought of 1987 to 1992 and by MWD price increases. Its Mission Basin Groundwater Purification Plant does not directly desalt the ocean but pulls groundwater affected by seawater intrusion. The plant currently can produce 2.2 million gallons per day (seven percent of the city's needs), but it is being expanded to handle six million gallons per day.

Farther down the coast, the city of Carlsbad and the San Diego County Water Authority are preparing to desalinate ocean water at the Cabrillo Power Plant in Carlsbad and at a second plant in Chula Vista. The Cabrillo plant is coupled with an existing power plant that already has seawater intakes for cooling. It should produce 9.3 percent of San Diego County's domestic supply.

The cost of desalination, compared to other water sources, has kept the technique from widespread use, but costs have come down in recent years, as new membranes have been developed for reverse-osmosis technology. In reverse-osmosis systems, water is forced under pressure through semipermeable membranes. Large molecules of salt (and contaminants) are held back; the smaller water molecules pass through. Ten years ago the membranes cost $1,200 and only lasted three years. Costs have dropped to about $450, and the new membranes should last 10 years. The MWD gives its member agencies subsidies of $250 per acre-foot to encourage the production of water from local sources, such as seawater, and to help the developing technology to compete with wholesale prices for imported water.

Desalination has substantial impacts that many people have not recognized. The process requires lots of energy; each

Plate 121. Waste from a desalination plant in Kuwait. Seawater desalination produces 75 percent of Kuwait's water supply. After treatment, concentrated brine wastewater is returned to the sea, where it mixes into the Persian Gulf, creating the shape of a tentacled monster. © Yann Arthus-Bertrand "Earth from Above"

acre-foot uses from 2,500 to 29,500 kilowatt-hours of electricity. It takes 100 gallons of seawater to produce 15 to 50 gallons of freshwater. Along with freshwater, a concentrated brine waste is generated. (Pl. 121.) Oceanside sends its brine 1.6 miles offshore. If desalination operations were to proliferate along the California coast, there would be impacts on the offshore water where the wastes were returned to the sea. Experience with other uses of the ocean as a depository for wastes ought to make Californians leery of the idea that the sea can absorb anything and everything we send it. From DDT lingering in the Channel Islands, put there by the Los Angeles

County sewer outfall, to plumes creeping inshore toward Orange County beaches from sewage piped 4.5 miles offshore, humanity's ability to damage coastal ecosystems has been repeatedly demonstrated. As always, the scale of the activities and depositions will determine their impacts.

Like groundwater, seawater can be a local supply source that does not require rivers to be dammed and long-range aqueducts to be built. Tapping into the "endless" ocean is an attempt to make water limits irrelevant. If we succeed, the question becomes, do we really want the unlimited growth that could be accommodated with "unlimited" water?

# What Future Do You Choose?

Every five years the California Department of Water Resources updates the California Water Plan. The next update will be completed in 2003. The 1998 version estimated that demand exceeded supply by 1.6 million acre-feet in average water years and 5.2 million acre-feet in drought years. Based on a population projected to grow to 47.5 people by 2020, drought year shortfalls would increase to 6.2 million acre-feet by 2020. (Map 26.) Projections such as these have been used to justify water development projects ever since the first California Water Plan was prepared in 1957. Used that way, the population estimates become self-fulfilling prophecies.

The first water plan focused on how to fully develop the state's water resources. Today the focus has shifted toward water management. The difference has been characterized as "concrete versus the soft path." One new emphasis is encouragement of increased dependence on local water supplies, rather than on long-distance transfers. In addition, the logic of focusing on dry years when estimating available water supply seems to have penetrated. Planning development based on water available in "average" years will lead to certain shortages, given the reality of droughts in California's historic cli-

0
**194**
North
Coast

10
**128**
North
Lahontan

85
**989**
Sacramento
River

Map 26. Water shortages
forecast for 2020, with existing facilities and programs (thousands of acre-
feet). (Redrawn from
California Department of
Water Resources 1998.)

63
**711**
San Joaquin
River

0
**287**
San
Francisco
Bay

720
**1,851**
Tulare
Lake

270
**308**
South
Lahontan

172
**270**
Central
Coast

147
**158**
Colorado
River

944
**1,317**
South
Coast

mate pattern. For the first time, the 2003 update will address
climate change and consider strategies for coping with global
change.

The water plans contain fascinating facts and trends but
can sometimes make for heavy reading. They are full of the
special language of abbreviations and acronyms ("waters-
peak," it might be called) that professionals adopt. Passages
like this, from the 1998 update, may require a translator:
"SEWD holds a contract for 75 TAF/yr of interim supply from
New Melones. CSJWCD has CVP contracts for 80 TAF/yr, 31
TAF of which is interim supply."

Despite the identification of shortages, there *is* lots of
water in California. There is enough water to serve populations far greater than today's; we could grow to well over 200
million people, if that is our choice. That would require taking water from its current uses in the environment or agricul-

ture. Whether we want to facilitate such a conversion, and whether anyone would want to live in that California, under those conditions, are the real questions. The authors of the California Water Plan will not answer them for us, but simply identify options.

Ever since World War II, California's urban centers and freeway-centered lifestyle have fostered sprawling growth in a succession of "booms" that were *only* sustained because of long-distance water delivery systems. Regions such as Southern California overcame regional limits with imported water (pl. 122). Today there are about 18 million people in Southern California, where local water sources could have sustained only three million. Similar population growth happened in the San Francisco Bay Area. Silicon Valley, the computer industry center that fostered development across the Santa Clara Valley and regional bedroom communities, also generated a voracious thirst for industrial and domestic water, all delivered in the Hetch Hetchy, Mokelumne, and California Aqueducts.

Pressures for continued urban growth are the greatest threats to long-term agricultural production and meaningful environmental protection in California. Recent commitments of water to the environment are actually not new "demands" on supply, but belated recognition that too much essential water was taken away in the past. Agricultural demand is contracting now, in part through better conservation practices, but also as prime farmland is relentlessly paved over. The future increases in "demand" predicted by water planners are based primarily on uncontrolled urban population growth.

"Economic growth, of course, depends on population growth," a *San Francisco Chronicle* editorial told its readers on August 6, 1989. "Population growth depends absolutely on guaranteed—and continuing and growing—supplies of good quality drinking water." That has been the dogma that shaped the evolution of the California dream. There has been almost

Plate 122. Los Angeles. "Whoever brings the water, brings the people" (William Mulholland).

no room within that belief system for contemplation of long-term sustainability, carrying capacity, or optimal growth limits.

Until recently, there was no legal requirement that sufficient water be available before new developments were permitted. Despite fierce opposition from real estate and development interests, in 2001 the California legislature finally required such common sense. Now there must be assurances of adequate water supplies before large developments (more than 500 units) can be approved. Whether the measures will be effective depends on whether they simply spawn a host of 499-unit projects or are circumvented by water providers like the MWD, which has promised to acquire whatever water is needed for any future growth. Such folly has been the historic pattern in California's water history, yet the time may have come for fundamental change.

An alternative would be to live within our means and seriously discuss how best to achieve long-term sustainability that preserves the abundance of life in California. If we insist on continuing the historic pattern, effects on the environ-

Plate 123. Water: the lifeblood of the Golden State. This photograph is of Bubbs Creek.

ment and on our quality of life must worsen, despite our best efforts at habitat and species protection, and despite concepts like "smart growth." Never-ending growth, whether smart or dumb, will inevitably overtake the limits of California's water systems.

William Mulholland, the engineer behind the Los Angeles Aqueduct, once said, "Whoever brings the water, brings the people." He was right. A corollary might be, "From wherever water is taken, life will be altered and diminished." Water is the essence of life in California, as it is everywhere on this planet (pl. 123). The life we in California choose, the future we choose, will continue to be shaped most of all by decisions about water.

# ACRONYMS AND ABBREVIATIONS

**AF** acre-foot; enough water to cover one acre to a depth of one foot; 325,851 gallons.
> 1 AF serves an average of 1 to 2 households or 5 to 8 people per year.
> MAF: million acre-feet
> TAF: thousand acre-feet

**APPMA** American Pet Products Manufacturers Association

**BMPs** Best Management Practices

**CAL-EPA** California Environmental Protection Agency

**CALFED** state and federal Bay Delta Program (1994)

**CEQA** California Environmental Quality Act (1970)

**CVP** Central Valley Project (federal)

**CVPIA** Central Valley Project Improvement Act (1992)

**CWA** Clean Water Act

**DFG** Department of Fish & Game (state)

**DWP** Department of Water and Power (Los Angeles); also LADWP

**DWR** Department of Water Resources (state)

**EBMUD** East Bay Municipal Utility District

**EPA** Environmental Protection Agency (federal)

**ESA** Endangered Species Act (both state and federal)

**FERC** Federal Energy Regulatory Commission

**IID**  Imperial Irrigation District

**LADWP**  Los Angeles Department of Water and Power; also DWP

**MAF**  million acre-feet

**MTBE**  methyl tertiary butyl ether (gasoline additive, water pollutant)

**MWD**  Metropolitan Water District of Southern California; also SCMWD

**NPS**  non-point source (of water pollution)

**NRDC**  Natural Resources Defense Council

**PG&E**  Pacific Gas & Electric

**SDCWA**  San Diego County Water Authority

**SFPUC**  San Francisco Public Utilities Commission

**SWP**  State Water Project (since 1960, administered by DWR)

**SWRCB**  State Water Resources Control Board

**TAF**  thousand acre-feet

**TCE**  trichloroethylene (industrial solvent, water pollutant)

**TDS**  total dissolved solids (water treatment standard)

**THM**  trihalomethanes (chlorination by-product; health risk)

**TMDL**  total maximum daily load (specifies pollutant level allowed to meet water quality Standards)

**USBR**  United States Bureau of Reclamation

**USGS**  United States Geological Survey

**UV**  ultraviolet radiation (water treatment method)

# HISTORICAL TIMELINE

For more details see Norris Hundley Jr.'s *The Great Thirst: Californians and Water, 1770s–1990s* (2001). For environmental changes tied to the state's history of water development, see Carle's *Water and the California Dream: Choices for the New Millennium* (2003).

**1781**   Spanish settlers erect a dam on the Los Angeles River to serve the new Pueblo de Los Angeles.

**1848**   Alta California becomes the property of the United States under the Treaty of Guadalupe Hidalgo, which includes language to protect pueblo water rights as identified under Mexican law.

James Marshall discovers gold at Sutter's Mill on the south fork of the American River.

**1849**   Ninety thousand 49ers arrive in one year. They mine Sierra Nevada riverbeds first and later build ditches, flumes, and reservoirs to appropriate water for hydraulic mining.

Levees are constructed to try to confine waters in the San Francisco Bay–Delta.

**1850**   At statehood California's population is about 100,000. The Native American population has dropped to about 30,000 (down from about 300,000 before contact with Europeans).

**1861**   Extensive "swampland reclamation" is under way in the Central Valley, encouraged by federal and state laws.

**1870**   California farmers irrigate 60,000 acres.

The state's population is 560,000.

| 1874 | A federal commission appointed by President Ulysses S. Grant proposes a storage and distribution system for the Central Valley. |
|---|---|
| 1884 | A federal circuit court orders hydraulic mines to stop damaging downstream property owners with runoff sediments. This order effectively stops hydraulic mining. |
| 1887 | The Wright Act becomes state law, permitting formation of irrigation districts. |
| 1902 | President Theodore Roosevelt signs the Reclamation Act. The Bureau of Reclamation begins a series of investigations on control and use of the Colorado River. |
| | California has 2.6 million acres of irrigated farmland. |
| 1905 | The Colorado River breaks through Imperial Valley Canal headgates. After two years, the Southern Pacific Railroad is finally able to close the "leak," which has formed the Salton Sea. |
| | Los Angeles voters authorize bonds for the Owens Valley project to bring Owens River water to Los Angeles. |
| 1910 | San Francisco voters approve the Hetch Hetchy water project to bring Tuolumne River water from Yosemite National Park. |
| 1913 | The Los Angeles Aqueduct begins delivering Owens Valley water. |
| 1916 | In the Imperial Valley, 300,000 acres are being irrigated. |
| 1920 | The population of the city of Los Angeles reaches 576,000, surpassing that of San Francisco. |
| 1920–23 | Los Angeles buys more land and water rights in the Owens Valley. |
| 1922 | The Colorado River Compact apportions water between states. |
| 1923 | San Francisco's dam floods Hetch Hetchy Valley, though the aqueduct and tunnels will not deliver water to the city for another decade. |
| 1924 | Owens Valley residents blow up the Los Angeles Aqueduct; Owens Lake is dry due to water diversions. |

| 1927 | East Bay Municipal Utility District (EBMUD) begins building Mokelumne River aqueduct facilities. |
|---|---|
| 1928 | The Metropolitan Water District of Southern California (MWD) is formed; a campaign is launched to pass a bond act for a Colorado River aqueduct. |
| | The California Constitution is amended to mandate that water not be wasted, but put to reasonable and beneficial uses. |
| | St. Francis Dam, part of the Los Angeles water system, collapses, killing over 400 people. |
| 1929 | State, federal, and local agencies begin cooperative snowpack monitoring to forecast water supplies. |
| 1929–34 | California suffers its most severe drought since statehood. This drought becomes the standard for estimating needed storage capacity in reservoirs built later. |
| 1930 | EBMUD's Mokelumne River project is in service. |
| | The state's population reaches 5.5 million. |
| 1931 | Southern California voters approve a $220 million bond so the MWD can begin building the Colorado River Aqueduct. |
| | The County of Origin Law is passed, guaranteeing the right of counties to reclaim their exported water if they ever need it. |
| 1933 | Federal construction of Hoover Dam (the Boulder Canyon project) begins. |
| | The California legislature and, later, voters in a referendum approve the Central Valley Project Act and a construction bond, but the Great Depression keeps the state from financing the project. |
| 1934 | The Hetch Hetchy Aqueduct begins delivering Tuolumne River water to San Francisco (24 years after the project is authorized). |
| | The Bureau of Reclamation begins construction on Parker Dam, to impound water for the Colorado River Aqueduct, and on the All-American Canal, to deliver Colorado River water to the Imperial Valley. |

| **1936** | The federal Flood Control Act authorizes multipurpose dams, inaugurating an era of dam building across the West. |
| **1937** | The federal government takes over the Central Valley Project (CVP). |
| | Los Angeles voters pass a $40 million bond to build a Mono Basin extension to the Los Angeles Aqueduct and to buy more Owens Valley land. |
| **1938** | Shasta Dam construction begins as part of the CVP. It will create the state's largest reservoir. |
| **1940** | The All-American Canal begins delivering water to the Imperial Irrigation District (IID). |
| | The California population is 6.9 million. |
| **1941** | The MWD completes the Colorado River Aqueduct, bringing water 242 miles to Southern California. |
| | Water diversions from Mono Lake streams begin reaching Los Angeles. |
| **1942** | Imperial Valley farms receive the first deliveries via the All-American Canal. |
| **1943** | The Mexican-American Treaty guarantees Mexico 1.5 million acre-feet per year from the Colorado River. |
| **1945** | Construction begins on Friant Dam on the San Joaquin River, as part of the CVP. |
| **1948** | Construction begins on Folsom Dam on the American River, as part of the CVP. |
| **1950** | State Attorney General Edmund G. "Pat" Brown declares that federal CVP projects need not comply with state fish protection laws, calling such releases "a waste of water." |
| | Irrigated acreage is up to 6.5 million acres. |
| | About 80,000 pumps are extracting groundwater in California. |
| | The state's population is over 10.5 million. |
| **1951** | The first CVP deliveries via the Delta-Mendota Canal bring Sacramento Valley water south to the San Joaquin Valley. |

| | |
|---|---|
| **1960** | Voters pass a $1.75 billion bond act authorizing the State Water Project (SWP). |
| | California has more than eight million irrigated acres. |
| | The state's population is 15.7 million. |
| **1962** | The SWP begins construction of Oroville Dam on the Feather River. |
| **1963** | California becomes the nation's most populous state, passing New York. |
| **1966** | Construction of New Melones Dam begins on the Stanislaus River. |
| **1968** | Oroville Dam is dedicated, and the reservoir is filled to its capacity of 3.5 million acre-feet. The SWP makes its first deliveries of Northern California water to the San Joaquin Valley. |
| | The national Wild and Scenic Rivers Act becomes law. |
| **1969** | San Luis Reservoir is completed, a joint state/federal facility and the nation's largest off-stream reservoir. |
| **1970** | Owens Valley groundwater pumping and Mono Basin diversions increase to fill the second barrel of the Los Angeles Aqueduct. |
| | The National Environmental Quality Act, California Environmental Quality Act (CEQA), and California Endangered Species Act (ESA) are enacted. |
| | California is now the most urban state in the nation and still the most populous, at 20 million. |
| **1971** | The SWP's California Aqueduct begins moving northern water all the way to Southern California, pumping it nearly 2,000 feet over the Tehachapi Mountains. |
| | The California Wild and Scenic Rivers Act is passed, prohibiting new dams on North Coast rivers. |
| **1972** | The federal Clean Water Act passes, including provisions to protect wetlands. |
| | Inyo County sues Los Angeles under CEQA over groundwater and irrigation issues. |

| 1973 | The federal Endangered Species Act (ESA) is passed to protect species and critical habitats. |
|---|---|
| 1974 | The Safe Drinking Water Act sets federal drinking-water standards. |
| 1975 | Construction of Auburn Dam is suspended due to seismic concerns. |
| 1976–77 | California sees its driest year since record keeping began. |
| 1976–79 | A court rejects two Environmental Impact Reports (EIRs) prepared for Los Angeles's operation of a second aqueduct. |
| 1980 | Smith River and parts of the other last free-flowing rivers in Northern California are given federal Wild and Scenic Rivers status. |
| 1982 | A statewide vote rejects the Peripheral Canal, marking the first defeat of a major California water project. |
| 1983 | Deformed and dead waterfowl are found at Kesterson Reservoir; the cause is identified as toxic farm drainage.<br><br>The California Supreme Court rules that the Public Trust Doctrine applies to Mono Lake and that established water licenses must be modified when public trust values are being damaged. |
| 1985 | The Central Arizona Project comes on line; California stands to lose about 800,000 acre-feet a year of water it had been taking beyond its allowance. |
| 1987–93 | A six-year drought strikes California. |
| 1988 | The MWD and the IID sign a water transfer agreement; conservation in the Imperial Valley is to make up to 100,000 acre-feet per year available to the MWD. |
| 1989 | Winter-run Chinook Salmon *(Oncorhynchus tshawytscha)* receive emergency listing as threatened under the federal ESA and endangered under the California ESA. |
| 1990 | The state's population reaches 29.8 million. |
| 1991 | The California Drought Water Bank is created to meet short-term water needs by marketing agricultural water to cities. This measure is repeated in 1992 and 1994. |

| 1992 | The Central Valley Project Improvement Act returns 800,000 acre-feet of water to the environment each year. |
|------|---|
| | A federal district court rules that state law protecting fisheries does apply to the CVP. |
| 1993 | A court rules that the CVP must obey state law and keep water for fish below dams. |
| | The Delta Smelt *(Hypomesus transpacificus)* is declared a threatened species under the California ESA. |
| 1994 | The Bay-Delta Accord is signed, establishing the state/federal CALFED program to seek solutions to the problems of the San Francisco Bay–Delta. |
| | The state modifies Los Angeles's water licenses to protect public trust values at Mono Lake and its tributary streams. |
| | Winter-run Chinook Salmon are reclassified as endangered under federal law. |
| 1995 | Widespread flooding occurs in many California counties. |
| 1997 | The Coastal Branch of the SWP is completed to San Luis Obispo and Santa Barbara Counties. |
| | Winter floods set new records along the Sacramento and San Joaquin Rivers, with damage totaling over $2 billion in 48 counties. |
| 1998 | Los Angeles and the Great Basin Air Pollution Control Board agree to resolve Owens Lake dust storms by 2006. |
| | The IID negotiates to send 200,000 acre-feet a year to San Diego. (The controversial plan is still being debated in 2003.) |
| | DWR's California Water Plan update estimates the state's water shortages at 1.6 million acre-feet in average water years and 5.2 million acre-feet in drought years, and forecasts increased shortages by 2020. |
| 1999 | The MWD completes construction of the off-stream Diamond Valley Reservoir near Hemet and begins filling it with Colorado River and SWP water. |
| | Spring-run Chinook Salmon and coastal Chinook Salmon are listed as threatened under the federal and state ESAs. |

After courts rule that the dewatering of the San Joaquin River violated state law, negotiations begin to develop a river restoration plan.

**2000**    CALFED releases a plan to address the San Francisco Bay–Delta issues.

**2001**    State laws mandate, for the first time, that large new developments must not be approved unless adequate water supplies are available first.

**2002**    When California fails to meet a year-end deadline for a plan to gradually end its reliance upon surplus Colorado River water, the Department of the Interior responds with immediate cuts for the MWD and the IID.

The state's population is about 35 million.

# AGENCIES AND ORGANIZATIONS

**State of California**

Delta Protection Commission, www.delta.ca.gov

Department of Conservation, www.consrv.ca.gov

Department of Fish and Game, www.dfg.ca.gov/dfghome.html

Department of Food and Agriculture, www.cdfa.ca.gov

Department of Health Services, Division of Drinking Water and
Environmental Management,
www.dhs.cahwnet.gov/org/ps/ddwem

Department of Water Resources, www.water.ca.gov; Water Plan
update, www.waterplan/water.ca.gov

Environmental Protection Agency (CalEPA), www.calepa.ca.gov

Reclamation Board, www.recbd.ca.gov

San Francisco Bay Conservation and Development Commission,
http://ceres.ca.gov/bcdc

State Water Resources Control Board, www.swrcb.ca.gov

**Federal**

Army Corps of Engineers, www.usace.army.mil

Bureau of Land Management, www.blm.gov/nhp/index.htm

Bureau of Reclamation, www.usbr.gov

Environmental Protection Agency, www.epa.gov

Fish and Wildlife Service, www.fws.gov

Forest Service, www.fs.fed.us

Geological Survey, http://ca.water.usgs.gov;
http://sfbay.wr.usgs.gov

National Marine Fisheries Service, www.nmfs.noaa.gov

Natural Resources Conservation Service, www.ca.nrcs.usda.gov

Western Area Power Administration, www.wapa.gov

### Joint Federal/State

CALFED Bay-Delta Program, http://calfed.ca.gov

### Nongovernment

*A partial list*

American River Conservancy, www.coloma.com/arc/index.html
Audubon California, www.audubon-ca.org
Bay Institute of San Francisco, www.bay.org
California League of Conservation Voters,
    www.ecovote.org/ecovote
California Wild Heritage Campaign, www.californiawild.org
CalTrout, www.caltrout.org
Environmental Defense Fund, www.environmentaldefense.org
Friends of the Los Angeles River, www.folar.org
Friends of the River, www.friendsoftheriver.org
Friends of the Trinity River, www.fotr.org
Heal the Bay, www.healthebay.org
Mono Lake Committee, www.monolake.org
Natural Resources Defense Council, www.nrdc.org
Owens Valley Committee, www.ovcweb.org
Restore Hetch Hetchy, www.hetchhetchy.org
Santa Monica BayKeeper, www.smbaykeeper.org
Sierra Club, www.sierraclub.org
South Yuba River Citizens League, www.syrcl.org

### Water Resource Institutes and Research Centers

Center for Water Resources, UC Riverside,
    www.waterresources.ucr.edu
Water Education Foundation, www.water-ed.org
Water Resources Center Archives, UC Berkeley,
    www.lib.berkeley.edu/WRCA

# REFERENCES

American Farmland Trust. 1995. *Alternatives for future urban growth in California's Central Valley: The bottom line for agriculture and taxpayers.* Washington, D.C.: American Farmland Trust. October.

———. 1997. *Water policy and farmland protection.* Available at www.farmland.org/Farmland/files/water/execsum.htm.

Arthus-Bertrand, Yann, David Baker, Lester Russell Brown, and Jean-Marie Pelt. 1999. *Earth from Above.* New York: Harry N. Abrams.

Bakker, Elna. 1984. *An island called California.* Berkeley: University of California Press.

Ball, Philip. 2001. *Life's matrix: A biography of water.* Berkeley: University of California Press.

Barlow, Maude, and Tony Clarke. 2002. *Blue gold: The fight to stop the corporate theft of the world's water.* New York: New Press.

Bay Institute of San Francisco. 1998. *From the Sierra to the sea: The ecological history of the San Francisco Bay–Delta watershed.* San Rafael, Calif.: The Bay Institute of San Francisco.

Blomquist, William A., and Elinor Ostrom. 1992. *Dividing the waters: Governing groundwater in Southern California.* Lanham, Md.: Institute for Contemporary Studies.

Brechin, Gray. 1999. *Imperial San Francisco: Urban power, earthly ruin.* Berkeley: University of California Press.

Bryant, Edwin. [1848] 1985. *What I saw in California.* Lincoln: University of Nebraska Press.

CALFED Bay-Delta Program. 1998. Executive summary of *Draft programmatic environmental impact statement/environmental impact report.* Sacramento.

———. 2002. *CALFED Bay-Delta Program annual report, 2001.* Revised. Sacramento.

California Dams Database, Berkeley Digital Library Project. N.d. Available at http://elib.cs.berkeley.edu/dams/dam-map.html.

California Department of Conservation. 2000. *Farmland conversion report, 1998–2000.* Sacramento.

California Department of Fish and Game. 2002. *Threatened and endangered fishes, list and species account.* Sacramento. Available at http://www.dfg.ca.gov/hcpb/species/t_e_spp/tefish/tefisha.shtml.

California Department of Fish and Game. N.d. Available at www.dfg.ca.gov/lands/fish1.html.

California Department of Water Resources. 1993. *Water facts: Ground water.* Sacramento.

———. 1996. *California State Water Project.* Sacramento.

———. 1998. *Bulletin 160–98: California Water Plan.* Sacramento.

———. 2003. *California Water Plan: Update.* Available at http://www.waterplan.water.ca.gov/b160/indexb160.html.

California State Water Resources Control Board. 1997. *California's rivers and streams: Working toward solutions.* Available at http://www.swrcb.ca.gov/riversst.htm.

———. 1999. *A guide to water transfers.* Sacramento: State Water Resources Control Board, Division of Water Rights, and California Environmental Protection Agency.

———. 2001. *Opportunity, responsibility, accountability: Nonpoint source pollution control program.* Sacramento: State Water Resources Control Board and California Environmental Protection Agency.

Carle, David. 2003. *Water and the California dream: Choices for the new millennium.* San Francisco: Sierra Club Books.

Carson, James H. [1852] 1931. *Early recollections of the mines, and a description of the great Tulare valley…steamer edition of the San Joaquin Republican.* Reprint, New York: W. Abatt.

Childs, Craig. 2000. *The secret knowledge of water.* Seattle: Sasquatch Books.

Cohen, Michael J., Jason I. Morrison, and Edward P. Glenn. 1999. *Haven or hazard: The ecology and future of the Salton Sea.* Oakland: Pacific Institute for Studies in Development, Environment and Security.

Cranham, Greg T., ed. 1999. *Water for Southern California.* San Diego: San Diego Association of Geologists.

Daniels, Tom, and Deborah Bowers. 1997. *Holding our ground: Protecting America's farms and farmland.* Washington, D.C.: Island Press.

Didion, Joan. 1979. *The white album.* New York: Farrar, Straus & Giroux.

Dinno, Rachel, ed. 1999. *Restoring the California dream: Ten steps to improve our quality of life.* Sacramento: Planning and Conservation League Foundation.

Duncan, David James. 2001. *My story as told by water.* San Francisco: Sierra Club Books.

Durrenberger, Robert W. 1968. *Patterns on the land.* Palo Alto, Calif.: National Press Books.

Eiseley, Loren. 1962. *The immense journey.* Chicago: Time-Life Books.

Field, C. B., G. C. Daily, F. W. Davis, S. Gaines, P. A. Matson, J. Melack, and N. L. Miller. 1999. *Confronting climate change in California.* Cambridge, Mass.: Union of Concerned Scientists; Washington, D.C.: Ecological Society of America.

Friends of the River. 1999. *Rivers reborn: Removing dams and restoring rivers in California.* Sacramento: Friends of the River.

Gottlieb, Robert, and Margaret Fitzsimmons. 1991. *Thirst for growth: Water agencies as hidden government in California.* Tucson: University of Arizona Press.

Hall, Clarence A. Jr., Victoria Doyle-Jones, and Barbara Widawski, eds. 1992. *The history of water: Eastern Sierra Nevada, Owens Valley, White-Inyo Mountains.* Vol. 4 of White Mountain Research Station Symposium. San Francisco: Regents of the University of California.

Hanson, Warren D. [1985] 1994. *San Francisco water and power.* San Francisco: City and County of San Francisco.

Hart, John. 1996. *Storm over Mono: The Mono Lake battle and the California water future.* Berkeley: University of California Press.

Hoffman, Abraham. 1981. *Vision or villainy? Origins of the Owens Valley–Los Angeles water controversy.* College Station: Texas A&M University Press.

Holder, Charles Frederick. 1906. *Life in the open: Sport with rod, gun, horse and hound in Southern California.* New York: Putnam's.

Hundley, Norris Jr. 2001. *The great thirst: Californians and water, 1770s–1990s.* Berkeley: University of California Press.

Kahrl, William L. 1979. *The California water atlas.* Sacramento: California Governor's Office of Planning and Research.

———. 1982. *Water and power.* Berkeley: University of California Press.

Kattelmann, Richard. 1996. Hydrology and water resources. In *Status of the Sierra Nevada: Sierra Nevada Ecosystem Project,* Vol. 2, *First report to Congress.* Davis: University of California, Davis, Centers for Water and Wildland Resources.

Kelley, Robert. 1989. *Battling the inland sea.* Berkeley: University of California Press.

Kolpin, Dana W., Edward T. Furlong, Michael T. Meyer, E. Michael Thurman, Steven D. Zaugg, Larry B. Barber, and Herbert T. Buxton. 2002. Pharmaceuticals, hormones, and other organic wastewater contaminants in U.S. streams, 1999–2000: A national reconnaissance. *Environmental Science Technology* 36 (6):1202–11.

Lehner, Peter, George P. Aponte Clark, Diane M. Cameron, and Andrew G. Frank. 1999. *Stormwater strategies: Community responses to runoff pollution.* New York: Natural Resources Defense Council.

Lemly, A. Dennis. 1997. Environmental implications of excessive selenium: A review. *Biomedical and Environmental Sciences* 10:415–35.

Leopold, Aldo. [1966] 1974. *A Sand County almanac.* New York: Sierra Club/Ballantine Books.

Leopold, A. Starker. 1984. *Wild California: Vanishing land, vanishing wildlife.* Berkeley: University of California Press.

Los Angeles Department of Water and Power. 1988. *Sharing the vision: The story of the L.A. Aqueduct.* Los Angeles.

Lufkin, Alan. 1991. *California's salmon and steelhead: The struggle to restore an imperiled resource.* Berkeley: University of California Press.

Mahoney, Laura. 2001. *Layperson's guide to agricultural drainage.* Sacramento: Water Education Foundation.

Mayer, Jim. 1996. *Layperson's guide to water pollution.* Sacramento: Water Education Foundation.

McClurg, Sue. 1998. Saving the salmon. *Western Water* (January/February): 4–13.

———. 2000a. The Mojave River basin decision. *Western Water* (September/October).

———. 2000b. *Water and the shaping of California.* Sacramento: Water Education Foundation.

———. 2001. Conjunctive use: Banking for a dry day. *Western Water* (July/August).

Metropolitan Water District of Southern California. 1997. *Wheeling: Gearing for the future of water marketing.* Los Angeles.

Miller, M.A., I.A. Gardner, C. Kreuder, D.M. Paradies, K.R. Worcester, D.A. Jessup, E. Dodd, M.D. Harris, J.A. Ames, A.E. Packham, and P.A. Conrad. 2002. Coastal freshwater runoff is a risk factor for *Toxoplasma gondii* infection of southern sea otters *(Enhydra lutris nereis). International Journal for Parasitology* 32 (8):997–1006.

Montgomery, Gayle B. 1999. *Its name was M.U.D., Book II.* Oakland: East Bay Municipal Utility District.

Mount, Jeffrey F. 1995. *California rivers and streams.* Berkeley: University of California Press.

Muir, John. [1901] 1991. *Our national parks.* San Francisco: Sierra Club Books.

———. 1912. *The Yosemite.* New York: Century Company.

———. [1938] 1979. *John of the mountains: The unpublished journals of John Muir.* Edited by Linnie Marsh Wolfe. Madison: University of Wisconsin Press.

———. 1961. *The mountains of California.* New York: Doubleday /American Museum of Natural History.

Olson, Eric D. 1999. *Bottled water: Pure drink or pure hype?* New York: Natural Resources Defense Council.

Pets may be major cause of water pollution in urban areas. 1999. *ScienceDaily Magazine,* January 6. Available at http://www.sciencedaily.com/releases/1999/12/991206071651.htm.

Pollution prevention fact sheet: Animal waste collection. N.d. Available under Fact sheets, Pollution prevention, Residential prevention practices, Animal waste collection, at http://www.stormwatercenter.net.

Reisner, Marc. 1986. *Cadillac desert: The American West and its disappearing water.* New York: Viking Penguin.

———. 1997. *Water policy and farmland protection: A new approach to saving California's best agricultural lands.* American Farmland Trust. Available at www.farmland.org/Farmland/files/water/cff .htm.

Rockwell, Robert L. 2002. *Giardia lamblia* and giardiasis, with particular attention to the Sierra Nevada. *Sierra Nature Notes.* Available at http://www.yosemite.org/naturenotes/Giardia.htm.

Rothenberg, David, and Marta Ulvaeus, eds. 2001. *Writing on water.* Cambridge: Massachusetts Institute of Technology, Terra Nova.

San Francisco Public Utilities Commission. N.d. *Hetch Hetchy Regional Water System.* Available at sfwater.org/detail.cfm/MC_ID /5/MSC_ID/52/MTO_ID/NULL/C_ID/555.

Santa Barbara, City of. N.d. *Water supply sources/desalination.* Available at http://ci.santa-barbara.ca.us/departments/public_works /water_resources/bfsupply.html#Desal.

Sax, Joseph L. 2002. *Review of the laws establishing the SWRCB's per-*

mitting authority over appropriations of groundwater classified as subterranean streams and the SWRCB's implementation of those laws. SWRCB No. 0–076–300–0. Sacramento: State Water Resources Control Board.

Schoenherr, Allan A. 1992. *A natural history of California.* Berkeley: University of California Press.

Shigley, Paul. 2002. Cities pressure San Francisco to repair Hetch Hetchy. *California Planning and Development Report* 17 (4) (April). Archived at http://www.cp-dr.com.

Snyder, Gary. 1995. *A place in space.* Washington, D.C.: Counterpoint.

Spriggs, Elisabeth Mathieu. 1931. The history of the domestic water supply of Los Angeles. Master's thesis, University of Southern California.

Stegner, Wallace. 1985. *The sound of mountain water.* Lincoln: University of Nebraska Press.

———. 1992. *Where the bluebird sings to the lemonade springs.* New York: Random House.

Steinbeck, John. [1952] 1995. *East of Eden.* New York: Viking Penguin.

Stene, Eric A. 1998. *The Central Valley Project.* Available on U.S. Bureau of Reclamation Internet site, http://www.usbr.gov/history /cvpintro.htm.

Stine, Scott. 1994. Extreme and persistent drought in California and Patagonia during mediaeval time. *Nature* 369 :546–49.

Storer, Tracy I., and Robert L. Usinger. 1963. *Sierra Nevada natural history.* Berkeley: University of California Press.

Svete, Stephen. 2002. Cheaper, better desalination gets a fresh look. *California Planning and Development Report* 17 (2) (February). Archived at http://www.cp-dr.com.

Thelander, Carl G., ed. 1994. *Life on the edge: A guide to California's endangered natural resources.* Vol. 1, *Wildlife.* Berkeley: BioSystems Books.

Thornton, Joe. 2000. *Pandora's poison: Chlorine, health, and a new environmental strategy.* Cambridge: MIT Press.

Totten, Glenn. 1997. *Layperson's guide to water conservation.* Sacramento: Water Education Foundation.

Trim, Heather. 2001. *Beneficial uses of the Los Angeles and San Gabriel Rivers.* Los Angeles: Los Angeles and San Gabriel Rivers Watershed Council.

Twain, Mark. [1872] 1972. *Roughing it.* Berkeley: University of California Press.

U.S. Army Corps of Engineers, Sacramento District. 2002. *American River watershed, California: Long-term study. Final Supplemental Plan, Formulation Report/Environmental Impact Statement/Environmental Impact Report.* Sacramento.

U.S. Bureau of Reclamation. 1987. *Hetch Hetchy: A survey of water and power replacement concepts, prepared on behalf of the National Park Service by the Bureau of Reclamation, Mid Pacific Region.* Draft. Sacramento.

———. 1999. *Central Valley Project Improvement Act: Final programmatic environmental impact statement.* Sacramento.

———. 2000. *The Salton Sea restoration project: Opportunities and challenges.* Washington, D.C.

U.S. Environmental Protection Agency. 2000. *Methyl bromide phase out.* Washington, D.C.

U.S. Environmental Protection Agency, Region 9. 1999. *California dairy quality assurance program fact sheet, September 1999.* Available at www.epa.gov/region09/cross_pr/animalwaste/dairyfact.html.

U.S. Geological Survey. N.d. Access USGS-San Francisco Bay and Delta Team. Available at http://sfbay.wr.usgs.gov/access/IntegratedScience/IntSci.html.

Walton, John. 1992. *Western times and water wars.* Berkeley: University of California Press.

Warshall, Peter. 1994. Streaming wisdom: Watershed consciousness in the twenty-first century. *River Voices.* Portland: River Network. Summer. Available at http://csf.Colorado.edu/bcwatershed/BNC1a.htm.

Water Education Foundation. 1991. *Colorado River Water Map.* Sacramento: Water Education Foundation.

———. 1994. *The water awareness guide: Where your water comes from.* Sacramento: Water Education Foundation.

———. 1997. *Layperson's guide to California water.* Sacramento: Water Education Foundation.

Williams, A. K., D. E. Prudic, and I. A. Swain. 1969. *Groundwater flow in the Central Valley, California.* U.S. Geological Survey professional paper 1401-D. Available at http://capp.water.usgs.gov/gwa/ch_b/gif/b093.gif.

Worster, Donald. 1985. *Rivers of empire: Water, aridity, and the growth of the American West.* New York: Pantheon.

Yoshiyama, Ronald M., Eric R. Gerstung, Frank W. Fisher, and Peter B. Moyle. 1996. Historical and present distribution of Chinook Salmon in the Central Valley drainage of California. In *Status of the Sierra Nevada: Sierra Nevada Ecosystem Project*, Vol. 3, *Final report to Congress*. Davis: University of California, Davis, Centers for Water and Wildland Resources.

# PHOTO CREDITS

All photographs are by the author except as noted below.

Plates 3, 11, 12, 21: Photos by Richard Kattelmann.

Plates 13, 24, 27, 36, 39, 92, 95, 102, 117: Photos by Frank Balthis.

Plate 14: Photo courtesy of NASA.

Plates 15–17, 22, 26, 31, 38, 41, 49, 52, 53, 57–64, 70, 79–81, 84–86, 96, 111: Photos courtesy of California Department of Water Resources.

Plates 29, 37, 43: Photos courtesy of U.S. Fish and Wildlife Service.

Plates 44, 51, 73, 103, 118, 120: Photos courtesy of Mono Lake Committee (photos for plates 118 and 120 by Herley Jim Bowling).

Plate 45: Photo by Forbes, courtesy of County of Inyo, Eastern California Museum.

Plate 47: Photo by B. Moose Peterson.

Plate 48: Photo courtesy of San Bernardino County Museum.

Plate 54: Photo courtesy of California State Parks.

Plate 65: Photo courtesy of U.S. Bureau of Reclamation.

Plate 74: Photo courtesy of Yosemite Museum, Yosemite National Park.

Plate 77: Photo courtesy of San Francisco PUC.

Plate 89: Photos courtesy of Joe Skorupa, U.S. Fish and Wildlife Service.

Plate 93: Photo courtesy of Inland Empire Utilities Agency.

Plate 97: Photo courtesy of U.S. Bureau of Reclamation.

Plate 104: Photo courtesy of Los Angeles Department of Water and Power.

Plate 106: NASA Space Shuttle image, June 2002.

Plate 108: Photo courtesy of The Nature Conservancy, Cosumnes River Preserve (staff photo).

Plate 112: Photo by Rita Schmidt Sudman, Water Education Foundation.

Plate 121: Photo by Yann Arthus-Bertrand (Bertrand et al. 1999).

# INDEX

# ABOUT THE AUTHOR

David Carle worked as a California State Park ranger for 27 years. Among other books, he is author of *Water and the California Dream: Choices for the New Millennium* (2003) and *Burning Questions: America's Hundred Years War Against Nature's Fire* (2002).

| | |
|---|---|
| Series Design: | Barbara Jellow |
| Design Enhancements: | Beth Hansen |
| Design Development: | Jane Tenenbaum |
| Cartographer: | Bill Nelson |
| Composition: | Impressions Book and Journal Services, Inc. |
| Text: | 9.5/12 Minion |
| Display: | Franklin Gothic Book and Demi |
| Printer and binder: | Everbest Printing Company |

# CALIFORNIA NATURAL HISTORY GUIDES

# Field Guides

**Sharks, Rays, and Chimaeras of California**
David A. Ebert. Illustrations by Mathew D. Squillante
0-520-22265-2 cloth, 0-520-23484-7 paper

**Mammals of California**
Revised Edition. E.W. Jameson, Jr., and Hans J. Peeters
0-520-23581-9 cloth, 0-520-23582-7 paper

**Dragonflies and Damselflies of California**
Timothy D. Manolis
0-520-23566-5 cloth, 0-520-23567-3 paper

**Freshwater Fishes of California**
Revised Edition. Samuel M. McGinnis.
Illustrations by Doris Alcorn
0-520-23728-5 cloth, 0-520-23727-7 paper

**Trees and Shrubs of California**
John D. Stuart and John O. Sawyer
0-520-22109-5 cloth, 0-520-22110-9 paper

**Pests of the Native California Conifers**
David L. Wood, Thomas W. Koerber, Robert F. Scharpf, and
Andrew J. Storer
0-520-23327-1 cloth, 0-520-23329-8 paper

# Introductory Guides

**Introduction to Water in California**
David Carle
0-520-23580-0 cloth, 0-520-24086-3 paper

**Introduction to California Beetles**
Arthur V. Evans and James N. Hogue
0-520-24034-0 cloth, 0-520-24035-9 paper

**Weather of the San Francisco Bay Region**
Second Edition. Harold Gilliam
0-520-22989-4 cloth, 0-520-22990-8 paper

**Introduction to Trees of the San Francisco Bay Region**
Glenn Keator
0-520-23005-1 cloth, 0-520-23007-8 paper

## Introduction to Shore Wildflowers of California, Oregon, and Washington

Revised Edition. Philip A. Munz. Edited by Dianne Lake and Phyllis M. Faber. Introduction by Robert Ornduff
0-520-23638-6 cloth, 0-520-23639-4 paper

## Introduction to California Mountain Wildflowers

Revised Edition. Philip A. Munz. Edited by Dianne Lake and Phyllis M. Faber. Introduction by Robert Ornduff
0-520-23635-1 cloth, 0-520-23637-8 paper

## Introduction to California Desert Wildflowers

Revised Edition. Philip A. Munz. Edited by Diane L. Renshaw Phyllis M. Faber. Introduction by Robert Ornduff
0-520-23631-9 cloth, 0-520-23632-7 paper

## Introduction to California Spring Wildflowers of the Foothills, Valleys, and Coast

Revised Edition. Philip A. Munz. Edited by Dianne Lake and Phyllis M. Faber. Introduction by Robert Ornduff
0-520-23633-5 cloth, 0-520-23634-3 paper

## Introduction to California Plant Life

Revised Edition. Robert Ornduff, Phyllis M. Faber, and Todd Keeler-Wolf
0-520-23702-1 cloth, 0-520-23704-8 paper

## Introduction to Horned Lizards of North America

Wade C. Sherbrooke
0-520-22825-1 cloth, 0-520-22827-8 paper

# Regional Guides

## Sierra Nevada Natural History

Revised Edition. Tracy I. Storer, Robert L. Usinger, and David Lukas
0-520-23277-1 cloth, 0-520-24096-0 paper